The Private Life of
VICTORIA

The Private Life of
VICTORIA

Queen, Empress,
Mother of the
Nation

ALEXANDER MACDONALD

ARCTURUS

ARCTURUS

This edition published in 2018 by Arcturus Publishing Limited
26/27 Bickels Yard, 151–153 Bermondsey Street,
London SE1 3HA

ISBN: 978-1-78888-316-0
AD006381UK

Printed in China

CONTENTS

Introduction
Victoria's Secrets **7**

Chapter One
Born to be Queen **13**

Chapter Two
The Kensington System **25**

Chapter Three
Ascending the Throne **37**

Chapter Four
Reginamania **47**

Chapter Five
The Bedchamber Crisis **55**

Chapter Six
The Adoration of Albert **65**

Chapter Seven
Married Life **81**

Chapter Eight
Albert Ascendant **91**

Chapter Nine
The Model Family **103**

Chapter Ten
Under Threat **117**

Chapter Eleven
My Duty… As a Woman **131**

Chapter Twelve
Widowhood **143**

Chapter Thirteen
Final Favourites **153**

Chapter Fourteen
The Grandmother
of Europe **169**

Index **189**

Introduction

VICTORIA'S SECRETS

The funeral of Queen Victoria on Saturday 2 February 1901 was a very public affair, but it spoke volumes about her private life. On a bitterly cold day, with snow swirling in the air, more than a million people turned out on the streets of London and Windsor to pay their respects. Despite the numbers, people were eerily silent as the coffin passed by, the only sound being the muffled drums and the gun salutes fired at regular intervals in Hyde Park. The writer John Galsworthy recorded, 'People gasped at the sight of the Queen's white-palled coffin as it passed – a mourning groan… unconscious, primitive, deep and wild.'

The words of another observer, Lady St Helier, were even more poignant. 'I was fairly taken by surprise which seized me by the throat, when the low gun carriage hove into sight,' she said. 'The tiny coffin draped in softest white satin – the whole thing so pure, so tender, so womanly, so suggestive of her who lay sleeping within – that every heart, one felt, must needs go out to meet her.' 'We all feel a bit motherless today,' wrote novelist Henry James. It was as though London was in mourning not just for its queen but for itself and the end of an era.

In her flower-bedecked coffin, she was hidden from view, much as she had been for most of her life since the death of her beloved husband Prince Albert 39 years earlier. The women mourners

Queen Victoria died at Osborne House on the Isle of Wight on 22 January 1901 and her body was brought to London for procession through the streets before being carried by train to Windsor.

wore black, as Victoria herself had done throughout her long widowhood.

Inside the coffin, she wore a white dress and her lace wedding veil. Beside her lay Prince Albert's dressing gown along with a shawl made by their long-dead second daughter, Princess Alice, a plaster cast of Prince Albert's hand, mementoes of virtually every member of her extended family, her servants and friends, including an array of shawls and handkerchiefs, framed photographs, lockets and bracelets, and a sprig of heather from Balmoral. On her hands were five rings given to her by Albert, her mother, her half-sister Feodora and her daughters Louise and Beatrice, and the gold wedding ring that once belonged to the mother of her gillie, John Brown, which she had worn since his death.

Framed photographs of Albert, her children and grandchildren were put in the coffin for good measure, along with a colour photograph of John Brown in a leather case plus some locks of his hair. Other photographs of Brown, which she used to carry with her, were to hand and even his handkerchief was laid upon her.

After the funeral service at St George's Chapel in Windsor, the coffin remained in the Albert Memorial Chapel until 4 February when she was laid to rest beside her beloved husband in the Romanesque mausoleum at Frogmore, adjoining Windsor Castle. In attendance were many members of her extended family.

Well connected

As royalty, these people were public figures, but behind closed doors they all played a part in the private life of the woman who came to be called the 'Grandmother of Europe'. Among the party were her sons Bertie, recently crowned King Edward VII, and Prince Albert, Duke of Connaught, along with her grandsons Kaiser Wilhelm II of Germany in the uniform of a British field marshal, his brother Prince Henry of Prussia and the Prince of Wales, later George V, with his son, then Prince Edward of York and later, briefly, Edward VIII. Also in attendance were Victoria's daughters, Princess Beatrice of Battenberg, Princess Helena of Schleswig-Holstein, Princess Louise, Duchess of Argyll, and Princess Victoria, formerly German Empress and Queen of Prussia, along with her granddaughter Princess Maud of Denmark. Victoria's elder cousin King Leopold II of the Belgians, Archduke Franz Ferdinand of Austria and Tsarevich Michael, the brother-in-law of Victoria's pretty granddaughter Alix, were also there, along with a handful of other crowned heads of Europe who were related to Victoria in one way or another.

After the Queen had been laid to rest, the statues and private memorials that Victoria had created for Brown were destroyed on the orders of Edward VII. Brown, who had been her closest confidant after the death of Prince Albert, had been replaced in Victoria's affections by her Indian servant Abdul Karim when Brown died in 1883. After her death, his home at Frogmore Cottage was raided and their correspondence burnt. Karim and his family were promptly evicted and sent back to India, which had long been the jewel in Victoria's crown.

Victoria is the second-longest-reigning monarch after Elizabeth II and she ruled at the height of Britain's power on the world stage. Although numerous wars had been fought in the name of the ever-expanding British Empire, Victoria herself was seen as a symbol of stability and domesticity both at home and abroad. When she was born, 91 years earlier, the country had just been victorious in the Napoleonic Wars and Bonaparte was safely locked up on the island of St Helena. With her as the national figurehead, Britain had developed the only truly industrialized economy and was the world's foremost naval power. In the 99-year *Pax Britannica* when

Britain took on the role of global policeman, which lasted until the First World War, the empire grew without cease until it ringed the whole world.

Against this background of ritualized pomp and power, Victoria was a passionate woman who led an often turbulent private life. And once she was dead, Edward VII, whose youthful indiscretions Victoria blamed for the death of Prince Albert, reverted to the dissolute ways of Victoria's Georgian forebears. At his coronation, his numerous mistresses occupied a gallery above the chancel in Westminster Abbey known as 'the King's loose-box'.

Meanwhile, two old Etonians, Arthur Benson and Lord Esher, set about editing Queen Victoria's letters, deleting anything that might have been considered, in those days, compromising or distasteful on the one hand, or even mildly affectionate on the other. Victoria's youngest daughter Princess Beatrice was charged with doing the same thing with her mother's diaries and other papers, copying out sections she deemed suitable for historical record, while destroying the originals. This task was still going on in May 1943, when she wrote to Victoria's great-grandson George VI, saying: 'You may not know that I was left my Mother's library executor, & as such, I feel I must appeal to [you to] grant me the permission to destroy any painful letters. I am her last surviving child & feel I have a sacred duty to protect her memory. How these letters can ever have been… kept in the Archives, I fail to understand.'

Victoria had remained on the throne through times of revolution, surviving rapid social change and eight assassination attempts, while Beatrice had lived through the Great War and seen many of the royal houses of Europe fall. For her, it was vital to keep the image of the Queen-Empress pristine. For all time, Victoria must remain the virtuous and selfless monarch. Fortunately, some copies of her most intimate private papers survived.

Chapter One

BORN TO BE QUEEN

Victoria was the last of the Hanoverian dynasty that had begun in 1714 when George I, the Elector of Hanover in Germany, was selected to succeed his second cousin Queen Anne, who died with no living offspring. Although there were others with greater claims to the British throne by primogeniture, he was the first Protestant in line. The others, all Roman Catholics, were prohibited from inheriting the throne by the Act of Settlement, which was passed in 1701. George left his wife behind in Germany, incarcerated in Ahlden Castle, Lower Saxony, after she was suspected of having an affair with a Swedish count, who was then murdered. George arrived in England with two mistresses, one tall and thin, the other short and fat and mocked respectively as 'the maypole and the elephant'.

His son, George II, didn't do much better. Although very much in love with his wife, he felt it was his royal duty to take mistresses. His frequent trips back to Hanover to indulge himself with the local prostitutes made him unpopular in Britain. George II's son Frederick was similarly debauched, but died before he could succeed his father.

In 1760, the throne passed to George III, who lived a more virtuous life. He and his wife, Charlotte of Mecklenburg-Strelitz, had 15 children, but he suffered from periodic bouts of madness, now thought to be the result of the blood disease porphyria. In an attempt to clean up the royal family's reputation, he signed the Royal Marriages Act of 1772. This stipulated that his descendants could not marry, legally, without the consent of the monarch and the approval of parliament. In practice, its effect was to give the princes a convenient excuse to wriggle out of any commitment to their lovers. As a result, they produced plenty of illegitimate children – 56 in all – none of whom were eligible to ascend the throne.

Separate lives

George III's eldest son George IV, who served as Prince Regent when his father was incapacitated, briefly abandoned his twice-widowed mistress Maria Fitzherbert, who he had married illegally, to wed Caroline of Brunswick in 1795. The marriage, forced on him by his father who agreed to pay off the Prince's mounting debts in return, was a disaster. The two were ill suited and soon hated each other, living completely separate lives. In 1814 Caroline left England to live in continental Europe. However, she chose to return for her husband's coronation in 1821, hoping to assert her rights as Queen Consort. But George IV refused to recognize her as queen and sought a divorce, a move that was unpopular with the public and soon abandoned. Despite this, he publicly banned her from attending his coronation on 19 July.

Caroline fell ill that day and died on 7 August. He was blamed. The only issue from their marriage was a daughter, Charlotte, born in 1796. Continued hostility between her parents plagued Charlotte's youth and adolescence. She was torn between a father she could respect but not love and a mother she could love but not respect. She once wrote: 'My mother was wicked, but she would not have turned so wicked had not my father been much more wicked still.'

Charlotte would have been queen if she had not died in 1817, aged 21, along with her stillborn child. At the insistence of parliament, George III's other sons quickly married in the hope that at least one of them would produce an heir.

Great expectations

The Prince Regent's younger brother William, Duke of Clarence, who later became William IV, had already had ten children with the actress Dorothea Jordan. On 11 July 1818, he married Princess Adelaide of Saxe-Meiningen, who at 25 was half his age. They had two daughters, who quickly died, and a number of stillborn children. Frederick, Duke of York, was estranged from his wife, Princess Frederica Charlotte of Prussia, who was already in her fifties and well past the age she could conceive.

The youngest son, Prince Adolphus, Duke of Cambridge, who served as Viceroy of Hanover, married Princess Augusta of Hesse-Cassel on 1 June 1818. One of their four children, Mary of Teck, became Queen Mary as the wife of George V. Then there was the notoriously louche and unpopular Ernest, Duke of Cumberland, who was even said to have had an incestuous relationship with his sister Princess Sophia, later the mother of an illegitimate child sired by her father's chief equerry. In 1815, Prince Ernest had married Princess Frederica of Mecklenburg-Strelitz, a divorcee. His mother, Queen Charlotte, disapproved and insisted that they live outside England. They had a son, who succeeded him as King of Hanover.

The fourth son, after George, Frederick and William, was Edward, the Duke of Kent, often regarded as the most intelligent of them all. Despite that, he had his weaknesses. A soldier, he had sired at least two illegitimate children by two different mothers. In response to his dalliances with the fairer sex, his father, George

III, sent him to Gibraltar in February 1790 in disgrace. However, there he was joined by his mistress, Julie de Sainte-Laurent, who he had met several years earlier in Geneva. Due to health problems caused by the hot Mediterranean weather, Edward only stayed in Gibraltar for six months. In a letter to his father, written in December 1790, he said: 'I petition that if it does not interfere with your commands for other Regiments in your service, you will allow me to be sent in the Spring with mine to any part of North America which you may chuse [*sic*] to appoint; allowing me, if it means with your approbation, to prefer Canada.'

Permission was granted and Edward travelled to Canada. Julie went with him. They were together for 28 years. Although they were thought to have no children, families in Canada claim descent from the couple. Returning to Gibraltar as Governor, this time Edward's severity provoked a mutiny. Three of the ringleaders were shot dead, a fourth flogged to death.

Like most of the sons of George III, Edward was profligate with money. The way to clear his debts was to give in to the urging of parliament and marry. When Edward proposed to the widowed Princess Victoria of Saxe-Coburg-Saalfeld, Julie only learned of his forthcoming nuptials from the newspapers. Princess Victoria had first married at the age of 17. With her husband Emich Carl, Prince of Leiningen, she had a son Carl and a daughter Feodora. Prince Emich died in 1814 and her brother Prince Leopold, the widower of George IV's daughter Charlotte, persuaded her to marry Prince Edward to secure the British succession.

The couple married in Coburg on 29 May 1818 and, again, at Kew Palace on 13 July. He was 52, she 32. They lived mainly in the moated castle at Amorbach near Frankfurt, Victoria's dower house, and raced back to England by coach when she was heavily pregnant, as Edward was convinced that, if his child was to succeed,

Princess Victoria Mary Louisa von Saxe-Coburg-Saalfeld was the mother of Queen Victoria. She was given the title Duchess of Kent.

it would be much more popular if it was born on British soil. The race for the succession was now going full tilt. Adelaide, the wife of his elder brother William, had just given birth to a daughter, who died after a few hours, while Augusta, the wife of younger brother Adolphus, had given birth to a healthy boy.

Fourth in line

Crossing the Channel in a gale, on the royal yacht reluctantly provided by the Prince Regent, Victoria was violently ill. Landing at Dover, she was taken to Kensington Palace, which had fallen into disrepair since the death of Queen Caroline, wife of George II, in 1737. There the recently honoured Duchess of Kent gave birth to a healthy girl on 24 May 1819.

At birth, the child was only fourth in line to the throne – behind the Prince Regent, the future George IV, the Duke of Clarence, the future William IV and her own father. And her succession was far from certain. It was not impossible that George or William would produce a legitimate heir, or that her own parents would have a boy that would displace her.

Nevertheless, the new-born girl almost immediately became a bone of contention between the Duke and Duchess of Kent and members of the Royal Court, a number of whom had children with a potential claim on the throne. At the last moment before the child's baptism, a low-key affair on 24 June 1819, the Prince Regent, a godfather, refused to allow her to be named Victoria Georgiana Alexandrina Charlotte Augusta, after her mother and godparents, as he would not have a derivative of his name being put before the Tsar's. But he eventually agreed to Alexandrina Victoria, after her godfather the Tsar – who had paid for her parents' marriage – and her mother. Both names were unpopular as they were deemed to be foreign. Until she was four, the child was known as 'Drina'. Later, attempts were made in parliament to change her name to Elizabeth or Charlotte, which were seen to be more English. They failed.

Starved of funds, Edward took his family to live in Sidmouth, Devon, where he died unexpectedly of pneumonia on 23 January 1820, after a long walk along the cliffs in a gale with his equerry John Conroy. Edward's only legitimate offspring, Victoria, was just eight months old. His father, George III, died six days later on 29 January, bringing the child two steps closer to the throne. Although Victoria was too young to know her father, her first prime minister Lord Melbourne told her that he was as agreeable as George IV and more 'posé' [a Regency term meaning 'sedate'] than William IV, without being as talkative. Plainly Victoria was swayed by this. She wrote in her journal on 1 August 1838: 'From all what I heard [sic] he was the best of all.' And although she had a difficult time with her mother, reading her diaries after she had died, Victoria wrote: 'All these notes show how very much She & my beloved Father loved each other!'

Although she could barely speak English, Victoria's mother now had the task of bringing up a child who was second in line to the throne. From the beginning, Victoria was headstrong, defying her teachers and those who looked after her. Even her beloved governess Louise Lehzen – a pastor's daughter from Coburg created baroness by George IV, so the future queen would not be nurtured by commoners – forced her to record her outbursts in a Conduct Book.

Country retreat
At the time of Victoria's birth, Kensington Palace was a venerable old building. Originally called Nottingham House, the structure was bought by William III in 1689 and enlarged by the architects

Christopher Wren and William Kent. Close to the hustle and bustle of the city surrounding it though set in 'intensely rural' gardens, the house functioned almost as a quiet country retreat. The family lived on two floors of a somewhat draughty, insect-ridden and partly derelict apartment. However, the slightly plump, promising and lively baby was indulged by compliant servants and fawned over by the great and the good who came to visit her. She flaunted her superiority over other youngsters and lacked true friends. But, despite being indulged with toys, clothes, pets, pony rides and trips to the seaside, she was unhappy, complaining later that she 'had no scope for my very violent feelings of affection – had no brothers and sisters to live with – never had a father – from my unfortunate circumstances was not on a comfortable or at all intimate or confidential footing with my mother… and did not know what a happy domestic life was.'

Indeed, apart from Baroness Lehzen, her only true companion was her half-sister Feodora; her half-brother Carl was at school in Switzerland at the time. But when Victoria was nine, Feodora married Ernst I, Prince of Hohenlohe-Langenburg, and left to live in Germany. Otherwise, she was always under the eye of adults – even at night when she slept in her mother's bedroom. She was not to walk up and down the stairs without holding someone's hand. And there were constant admonitions to sit up straight. A sprig of holly was pinned to the front of her dress to make her keep her chin up.

She was not yet 11 when she was leafing through a book on the kings and queens of England, where she discovered she was second in line to the throne. It is said that she burst into tears, later telling Prince Albert that she was 'very unhappy' at the discovery. However, it must already have been clear to her that she was in a unique position. From the age of seven she had been invited to the Royal Lodge at Windsor, where George IV lived with his mistress, Lady Elizabeth Conyngham. It was clear that the corpulent and dissolute king did not like her, but recognized her as the future of the monarchy.

George IV died on 26 June 1830 of 'obesity of the heart' – though alcoholism, gluttony and addiction to laudanum cannot have helped. 'There never was an individual less regretted by his fellow-creatures than this deceased king,' said *The Times*. And Victoria found herself first in line after William IV. She was dismayed and anxious.

Leading role

Lehzen claimed that, despite her distress at the prospect of becoming queen, Victoria was determined to rise to the role. While her education was all important, she would not let the thought crush her innate grit. Though she was diligent with her books, she also enjoyed tending flowers and dressing up. Otherwise she lavished affection on her dogs and played with her dolls, making over a hundred out of wood. With Lehzen, she painted and made clothes for them, so they resembled characters from the Court, ballet or opera, which she loved, and painstakingly listed each creation in a book. On 1 August 1832, she began keeping a diary, which she wrote in daily – apart from when she had just given birth – until the end of her life.

Occasionally, her loneliness was relieved by family visits. In June 1833, Feodora came to stay with her husband and two children. They had not seen each other for six years. When Feodora left seven weeks later, Victoria wrote: 'The separation was indeed dreadful. I clasped her in my arms, and kissed her and cried as if my heart would break, so did she, dearest sister. We then tore ourselves from each other in the deepest grief… When I came

Baroness Louise Lehzen (1784–1870), governess and tutor to Victoria.

home I was in such a state of grief that I knew not what to do with myself. I sobbed and cried most violently the whole morning... My dearest best sister friend, sister, companion all to me, we agreed so well together in all our feelings and amusements... I love no one better than her.'

Her other consolation was a surprisingly grown-up relationship and correspondence with her mother's brother, Uncle Leopold. Born in Coburg in 1790, Leopold was a German prince and member of the House of Saxe-Coburg and Gotha, a dynasty with influential connections to royal families all over Europe. After a career in the Russian army, during which he fought for the allies against Napoleon, he settled in London. In 1814, he had met Princess Charlotte, the daughter of George IV and Caroline of Brunswick, at a party in the Pulteney Hotel in Piccadilly. Charlotte, at the time the Prince Regent's only child, was second in line to the throne. Two years later, in March 1816, an announcement was made in the House of Commons that Charlotte and Leopold were to marry. They were granted £50,000 [£5 million in today's money or $6.5m] per year, bought Claremont House near Esher in Surrey and set up home there.

In one letter to 'Leo', as she called him, she remarked that she was studying the English sovereigns and their consorts as 'the history of my own country is one of my first duties'. An extract he sent her about Queen Anne showed her 'what a Queen ought not to be', so she wrote back asking that he send her something on 'what a Queen ought to be'. She also wrote to thank him for sending the autograph of Louis IV of France, and begged him for two more autographs – those of Madame de Sévigné, famed for the letters she wrote to her daughter, and that of the French playwright Racine, 'as I am reading the letters of the former, and the tragedies of the latter'.

She also visited him regularly in his house at Claremont and she and her mother would take seaside holidays with him in Ramsgate or Broadstairs in Kent. After the loss of his young bride Charlotte, Leopold continued to enjoy considerable status in Britain, giving his niece valuable lessons in statecraft. Victoria also became good friends with his second wife, Louise of Orléans, daughter of Louis-Philippe I, King of France. When they visited in 1835, Victoria said: 'She is delightful, and was so affectionate to me.'

Chapter Two

THE KENSINGTON SYSTEM

The most overbearing influence in Victoria's young life was that of Sir John Conroy, her father's former equerry who had become comptroller of the Duchess of Kent's household and inveigled his way into her confidence and affections. Both he and the Duchess were convinced that, although third in line behind the dukes of York and Clarence, Victoria would become queen and fervently hoped that she would ascend as a minor, so the Duchess could be regent and gather power and riches for herself and her dear friend Conroy. In an effort to exert control over the young Victoria's upbringing, Conroy kept her away from everyone except the Duchess and his relatives. His daughters were Victoria's only regular youthful companions.

With the succession crisis in full swing, contenders for the throne and their 'attendants' were busy manoeuvring into the best possible position, often by casting aspersions on others' claims. The Duchess was alarmed at reports that Ernest, Duke of Cumberland, who would have been the next brother in line for the throne, wanted rid of the young Victoria. He spread rumours that she was too weak to rule and might not even survive childhood. Another part of the 'Cumberland plot', as the Duke's plan was dubbed in the newspapers, was the circulation of a rumour that the Duchess of Kent was Conroy's mistress. When he dismissed

Baroness Späth, a close friend of Baroness Lehzen, from the household the story was that it was because she had witnessed 'familiarities' between Conroy and the Duchess. Victoria also feared that Conroy would sack Lehzen. However, plans to dismiss her were scuppered in 1835, when Lehzen nursed Victoria through a five-week illness, possibly tonsillitis, in Ramsgate, rendering herself irreplaceable.

In her journal, Victoria wrote: 'Dear good Lehzen takes such care of me and is so unceasing in her attentions to me that I shall never be able to repay her sufficiently for it but by my love and gratitude... She is the most affectionate, devoted, attached and disinterested friend I have, and I love her most dearly.'

Lehzen also supported the weakened Victoria when she refused to sign a document forced on her by her mother and Conroy that would give him the position of private secretary with a peerage when she became queen. She later told Lord Melbourne: 'All I underwent there; their (Ma's and JC) attempt (when I was still ill) to make me promise beforehand, which I resisted in spite of my illness, and their harshness – my beloved Lehzen supporting me alone.'

Play for power
Victoria loathed Conroy and he tried to isolate her from any outside influence. Other members of the royal family were concerned that he was not of sufficient rank for the position he occupied. But Conroy believed that his wife was the illegitimate child of Victoria's father. He instituted the strict 'Kensington system', which controlled every aspect of Victoria's young life and created a rival court developed at Kensington Palace, cut off from the lax morals of William IV, who referred to Conroy as 'King John'.

Sir John Conroy was comptroller of the Duchess of Kent's household. Victoria had him banished from the Royal Court in 1837.

William was already 64 when he came to the throne, the oldest person to take the crown of England, Scotland or Ireland, while Queen Adelaide was 38 and thought unlikely to produce any children. Victoria was still only 11 and parliament duly passed a Regency Act allowing for a regency should the King die before the next person in line for the throne reached the age of 18. While the prime minister, the Duke of Wellington, refused to allow the Duchess of Kent to take the title of Dowager Princess of Wales, she was to be named regent if William had no further legitimate heirs and died before Victoria was 18. An extra £10,000 [£1m/$1.3m in today's money] a year was provided for the future queen's education.

Conroy was determined to keep a grip on Victoria. He maintained his tyranny by pretending to be her protector. In response to Cumberland's machinations, Conroy accused him of wanting to have Victoria removed from the Duchess's care because she and Conroy were Whigs, while the rest of the royal family, including William, were Tories. When the 'plot' failed, Conroy claimed that Cumberland was trying to poison Victoria's milk, so he could become king. Victoria scoffed that this was 'Sir John's invention'. Even so, her milk was tasted each morning before breakfast.

On the up side, Conroy organized what the King mocked as 'Royal Progresses'. Victoria began to make royal tours so that she would get to know the country and the country would get to know her. The royal standard, crowns and loyal addresses were much in evidence. Although she was billeted comfortably with the aristocracy – both Tory and Whig – things she saw along the way shocked her. Outside Birmingham, she noted on 2 August 1832: 'We just passed through a town where all coal mines are and you see the fire glimmer at a distance in the engines in many places. The men, women, children, country and houses are all black. But I cannot by any description give an idea of its strange and extraordinary appearance. The country is very desolate everywhere; there are coals about, and the grass is quite blasted and black. I just now see an extraordinary building flaming with fire. The country continues black, engines flaming, coals in abundance, everywhere, smoking and burning coal heaps, intermingled with wretched huts and carts and little ragged children.'

She also mixed with the lowliest of her future subjects. On 1 January 1837, she spotted what she called 'a superior set of gypsies' camped near Claremont House.

'As we were walking along the road near to the tents, the woman who said she was called Cooper, who is generally the spokeswoman of the party, stepped across the road from the tents, & as we turned & stopped, came up to us with a whole swarm of children, six I think. It was a singular, & yet a pretty & picturesque sight,' she recorded. 'She herself with nothing on her head, her raven hair hanging untidily about her shoulders, while the set of little brats swarming round her, with dark dishevelled hair & dark dresses, all little things and all beautiful children... The gypsies are a curious, peculiar & very hardy race, unlike any other!'

Another, named 'Aunt Sarah', wished them a Happy New Year.

'I never saw "Aunt Sarah" look more beautiful than she did this time. I do so wish I could take a likeness of her, from nature. What a splendid study she would be! Lehzen gave her something, & they then loaded us with thanks & blessings.'

At the time, gypsies were looked down on, but Victoria said they were 'falsely accused, cruelly wronged, and greatly ill-treated'. She visited them several times, sketched them, sent them soup and sought to have their children educated. She also had food and blankets delivered when a gypsy woman gave birth. If asked, she said she would sponsor the fatherless child and call him Leopold.

William's complaint

Victoria did not attend the coronation of William IV on 8 September 1831. Her mother considered it a snub that her daughter would not be allowed to walk behind the King in his procession and made an excuse for her non-appearance by claiming the child had grazed her knee in a fall. The Duchess further defied the King by renovating the 17-room apartment they occupied in Kensington Palace against his orders. At a dinner at Windsor, William complained of the Duchess who was seated next to him, saying that he had 'been insulted – grossly and continuously insulted – by that person, but I am determined to endure no longer a course of behaviour so disrespectful to me'. He went on to complain that his niece had been kept from him. Victoria, who was also present, burst into tears. William had genuine affection for her, saying, as an old seadog: 'It will touch every sailor's heart to have a girl queen to fight for. They'll be tattooing her face on their arms, and I'll be bound they'll think she was christened after Nelson's ship.'

At 16, Victoria was just 4ft 11in and considered herself very fat. But then she began to grow slender and people noticed her large blue eyes. As she grew older, the regime in Kensington Palace slackened. She was allowed to choose her own hairstyle, read novels, learn Italian, take singing lessons and attend her mother's parties where she would dance with handsome young men. Rumours of her youthful infatuation with Lord Elphinstone, 12 years her senior, resulted in him being despatched to India as Governor of Madras.

Although she was no beauty, Victoria was, of course, considered a great catch. There were numerous other rumoured suitors, but her Uncle Leopold was keen for her to consider his nephew – and her first cousin – Prince Albert of Saxe-Coburg and Gotha. In

May 1836, the Duke of Coburg together with his two sons, Ernest aged 17 and Albert who was 16, paid a visit to England, spending nearly four weeks at Kensington Palace as guests of the Duchess of Kent. It was therefore natural that the two princes and Princess Victoria should spend time in each other's company, often visiting the attractions of the metropolis. Victoria wrote to Leopold telling him that she found Albert witty and fun, recording in her diary that he was 'extremely handsome; his hair is about the same colour as mine; his eyes are large & blue, & he has a beautiful nose, & a very sweet mouth with fine teeth; but the charm of his countenance is his expression, which is most delightful; *c'est a la fois*, full of goodness & sweetness, & very clever & intelligent.'

But Albert was also frail, and had a tendency to faint. In one letter to Leopold, she wrote: 'I am sorry to say that we have an invalid in the house in the person of Albert.' However, in another letter dated 7 June she said: 'I must thank you, my beloved Uncle, for the prospect of great happiness you have contributed to give me, in the person of dear Albert. Allow me, then, my dearest Uncle, to tell you how delighted I am with him, and how much I like him in every way. He possesses every quality that could be desired to render me perfectly happy. He is so sensible, so kind, and so good, and so amiable too. He has, besides, the most pleasing and delightful appearance you can possibly see.'

At the end of the month, he returned to Germany, but they continued writing to each other.

Financial independence

As Victoria's 18th birthday approached, the atmosphere in Kensington Palace grew tense. Conroy and the Duchess wanted Victoria to have any regency extended until she was 21 on the grounds that she was childish and immature, but she was obdurate.

Her half-brother, Carl of Leiningen, was brought in as a mediator, but he sided with Conroy.

Feeling for his niece, the King stepped in, promising her £10,000 [around £1 million in today's money – $1.3m] for her own use to give her the much-needed independence she craved. A letter with the news was sent by courier who had instructions to place it in Victoria's hand. But both her mother and Conroy tried to grab it. Eventually, Victoria was forced to read it to them. Her mother insisted that she reject the offer and Conroy wrote a formal reply asking, on account of Victoria's youth and inexperience, that the money go to her mother. For once cowed, Victoria dutifully copied it out in her own hand. But when William received it, he flung it aside in disgust, saying: 'Victoria has not written that letter.'

The 71-year-old king was already ailing. On 22 May 1837, his doctor Sir Henry Halford reported that he was 'in a very odd state and decidedly had the hay fever and in such a manner as to preclude his going to bed'. Lord Palmerston, then foreign secretary, wrote of the King being in 'a very precarious state… though he would probably rally'. However, it was clear that it was unlikely that he would live long. 'It is desirable he should wear the crown some time, however,' Palmerston added, 'for there would be no advantage in having a totally inexperienced girl of eighteen, just out of strict guardianship, to govern an empire.'

On 24 May 1837, Victoria's mood lightened. Celebrating her victory over her mother and Conroy, she recorded in her diary: 'Today is my 18th birthday! How old! and yet how far am I from being what I should be. I shall from this day take the firm resolution to study with renewed assiduity, to keep my attention always well fixed on whatever I am about, and to strive to become every day less trifling and more fit for what, if Heaven wills it, I'm someday to be!'

Outside a band began to play, concluding their recital with 'God Save the King'. That evening, she went to a ball, noting in her journal when she got home: 'The anxiety of the people to see poor stupid me was very great, and I must say I am quite touched by it, and feel proud which I always have done of my country and of the English Nation.'

Leopold sent his trusted advisor Baron von Stockmar to Kensington Palace to assess the situation. He reported back: 'I found the Princess fairly cool and collected, and her answers precise, apt and determined. I had throughout the conversation, the impression that she is extremely jealous of what she considers to be her rights and her future power and is therefore not at all inclined to do anything which would put Conroy into a situation to be able to entrench upon them. Her feelings seem, moreover, to have been deeply wounded by what she calls "his impudent and insulting conduct" towards her. Her affection and esteem for her mother seem likewise to have suffered by Mama having tamely allowed Conroy to insult the Princess in her presence, and by the Princess having been frequently a witness to insults which the poor Duchess tolerated herself in the presence of her daughter... O'Hum [Conroy] continues the system of intimidation with the genius of a madman, and the Duchess carries out all that she is instructed to do with admirable docility and perseverance... The Princess continues to refuse firmly to give her Mama her promise that she will make O'Hum her confidential adviser. Whether she will hold out, Heaven only knows, for they plague her, every hour and every day.'

On 13 June, the Duchess wrote to Victoria, saying: 'You are still very young and all your success so far has been due to your *Mother's* reputation. Do not be *too sanguine* in *your* own *talents* and *understanding*.'

The King's illness

Two days later, Victoria recorded in her journal: 'The news of the King is so very bad… I just hear that the doctors think my poor uncle the King cannot last more than forty-eight hours! Poor man! He was always kind to me, and he meant it well I know; I am grateful for it, and shall ever remember his kindness with gratitude.'

Lord Liverpool, a much-respected Tory and family friend, visited Kensington Palace in preparation for the expected succession. On his arrival, Conroy quickly made his pitch. He told Liverpool that Victoria was 'easily caught by fashion and appearance' and 'younger in her intellect than in years'. She would certainly need him as her private secretary when she became queen. Liverpool said that this was out of the question and offered him the position of keeper of the privy purse if he kept out of politics. Then Liverpool insisted on a private interview with Victoria.

'At about a ¼ p.2 came Lord Liverpool and I had a highly important conversation with him – alone,' she recorded. She agreed that she would have no private secretary and put herself in the hands of the prime minister, Lord Melbourne. Nor would she have Conroy as keeper of the privy purse. Did Liverpool not know of the 'many slights and incivilities' she had suffered at his hands, she asked? Liverpool's own daughter Lady Catherine Jenkinson had witnessed them, she said. Besides, Liverpool recorded in a memorandum: 'She knew things of him which rendered it totally impossible for her to place him in any confidential situation near her… which entirely took away her confidence in him… she knew of this herself without any other person informing her.'

She then showed Liverpool a letter dictated to Lehzen which, while respectful to the Duchess and firm concerning Conroy, said that Victoria refused to be bound by any promise she had made to them. The interview closed with Victoria asking Liverpool to speak to her two tormentors and 'open their eyes as to the difficulty of the situation in which they place me'.

For the next few days, Victoria stayed in her room and spoke only to Lehzen. Conroy consulted his friend, James Abercromby, speaker of the House of Commons, who said that, if Victoria would not listen to reason, 'she must be coerced'. Speaking in German so Conroy would not understand, Carl Leiningen begged his mother not to lock Victoria away as Conroy planned. Later Conroy told Leiningen that he had abandoned the use of coercion only because 'he did not credit the Duchess of Kent with enough strength for such a step'.

On 19 June, Victoria wrote to Leopold, saying: 'The King's state, I may fairly say, is hopeless; he may perhaps linger a few days, but he cannot recover ultimately. Yesterday the physicians declared he could not live till the morning, but today he is a little better; the great fear is his excessive weakness and no pulse at all... I feel sorry for him; he was always personally kind to me, and I should he ungrateful and devoid of feeling if I did not remember this.

'I look forward to the event which it seems is likely to occur soon, with calmness and quietness; I am not alarmed at it, and yet I do not suppose myself quite equal to all; I trust, however, that with goodwill, honesty and courage I shall not, at all events, fail. Your advice is most excellent, and you may depend upon it I shall make use of it, and follow it.'

Chapter Three

ASCENDING THE THRONE

On 20 June 1837, William IV died. Victoria recorded in her journal: 'I was awoke at 6 o'clock by Mamma, who told me that the Archbishop of Canterbury [William Howley] and Lord Conyngham [the Lord Chamberlain] were here, and wished to see me. I got out of bed and went into my sitting-room (only in my dressing-gown), and alone, and saw them. Lord Conyngham then acquainted me that my poor Uncle, the King, was no more, and had expired at 12 minutes p. 2 this morning, and consequently that I am Queen. Lord Conyngham knelt down and kissed my hand, at the same time delivering to me the official announcement of the poor King's demise. The Archbishop then told me that the Queen [Adelaide] was desirous that he should come and tell me the details of the last moments of my poor, good Uncle; he said that he had directed his mind to religion and had died in a perfectly happy, quiet state of mind, and was quite prepared for his death. He added that the King's sufferings at the last were not very great, but that there was a good deal of uneasiness. Lord Conyngham, who I charged to express my feelings of condolence and sorrow to the poor Queen, returned directly to Windsor. I then went to my room and dressed.

'Since it has pleased Providence to place me in this station, I shall do my utmost to fulfil my duty towards my country; I am very young and perhaps in many, though not in all things, inexperienced, but I am sure, that very few have more real goodwill and more real desire to do what is fit and right than I have.'

After breakfasting, she talked with Baron von Stockmar and wrote to Leopold and Feodora. Then she received a letter from the prime minister, saying he would come at nine.

'At 9 came Lord Melbourne, whom I saw in my room, and, of course, quite alone as I shall always do with my Ministers. He kissed my hand and I then acquainted him that it had long been my intention to retain him and the rest of the present Ministry at the head of affairs, and that it could not be in better hands than his. He then again kissed my hand. He then read to me the Declaration which I was to read to the [Privy] Council, which he wrote himself and which is a very fine one. I then talked with him some little longer time after which he left me. He was in full dress. I like him very much and feel confidence in him. He is a very straightforward, honest, clever and good man.'

She then wrote a letter of condolence to Queen Adelaide. At 11.30 she went downstairs for a meeting of the Privy Council in the red saloon. Melbourne asked if she would like him to walk with her into the room. She declined.

'I went in of course quite alone, and remained seated the whole time. My two Uncles, the Dukes of Cumberland and Sussex, and Lord Melbourne conducted me.'

She would soon be losing Uncle Ernest. The Salic Law in force in Germany barred the succession of a woman, so on the death of William, Cumberland became King of Hanover, a position handed down to the kings of England from George I, though the title changed from elector to king in 1814.

Taking up the reins

After taking her seat on the throne, Victoria read Melbourne's declaration and swore in the Privy Councillors. 'I was not at all nervous and had the satisfaction of hearing that people were satisfied with what I had done and how I had done it. Received after this, Audiences of Lord Melbourne, Lord John Russell, Lord Albemarle (Master of the Horse), and the Archbishop of Canterbury, all in my room and alone.'

Victoria's Privy Councillors praised their new queen unanimously. The Duke of Wellington said: 'She not merely filled the chair, she filled the room.' Lord Holland was quite smitten: 'Though not a beauty and not a very good figure,' he said, 'she is really in person, in face, an especially in eyes and complexion, a very nice girl and quite such as might tempt.'

Afterwards, she spoke with Stockmar. Melbourne visited again at nine that evening and remained for an hour: 'I had a very important and a very comfortable conversation with him. Each time I see him I feel more confidence in him; I find him very kind in his manner too,' she said.

Then she went downstairs to say goodnight to her mother. There was no mention of Conroy in the journal that day. However, Sir John had been at work. When Melbourne walked out of the Privy Council meeting wiping tears from his eyes, Baron Stockmar thrust into his hand a letter from Conroy. In it Sir John made a simple demand: 'My reward for the past, I conceive, should be a peerage – the red ribbon – and a pension from the Privy Purse of £3,000 a year.' This is worth £300,000 [$390,000] in today's money and more than any government minister received at the time. Melbourne dismissed his impudence and Victoria dismissed Conroy from her household, though he continued to serve her mother. To placate him, Melbourne promised to make him an

William Lamb, Lord Melbourne, was home secretary. He quickly gained Victoria's confidence and became her ally.

Irish peer. However, he would have to wait until an existing one died. When a vacancy eventually arose, Sir Robert Peel was prime minister and refused to honour Melbourne's promise.

The Duchess had also been working on Conroy's behalf. She wrote to Victoria asking if she could take Conroy to the proclamation. The Queen told her that it was Melbourne's decided opinion that he should not go. The Duchess replied: 'You do not know the world. S.J. [Sir John] has his faults, he may have made mistakes, but his intentions were always the best... This affair is much tattled and very unhappily. Take care, Victoria, you know your Prerogative! Take care that Melbourne is not King.'

Victoria wrote to Leopold, saying: 'My poor mother views Lord Melbourne with great jealousy.'

For then on, Victoria insisted that the Duchess follow etiquette. She would have to wait to be summoned before she could see her own daughter. Naturally, Victoria's prime minister had more privileged access.

Hard graft

The 18-year-old's capacity for work surprised her ministers who had served under two indolent kings. She rose at 8 a.m. to read the Bible and write despatches before breakfast with her mother at 10. Between 11 a.m. and 1.30 p.m. she saw her ministers, then she worked on her boxes and official papers, often late into the night. On 1 July 1837, she wrote in her journal: 'I have so many communications from the Ministers, and from me to them, and I get so many papers to sign every day, that I have always a very great deal to do; but for want of time and space I do not write these things down. I delight in this work. Wrote my journal. Did various things. Saw Lord Melbourne. At about ½ p.11 or a ¼ to 12 came Mr Spring Rice. Saw Lord John Russell. Wrote &c. At 2 came Sir Henry Wheatley to kiss hands upon being appointed my Privy Purse. At a little after 2 I saw Stockmar for a minute. At 10 minutes p.2 came Lord Palmerston and stayed till 6 minutes p.3. We talked about Russia and Turkey a good deal &c. He is very agreeable, and clear in what he says. Saw Stockmar for some time afterwards…'

But there were personal matters to attend to as well. '… I forgot to mention that I received a letter from dearest Aunt Louise in the morning. The children played in my room for a little while. At ½ p.5 I drove out with Mamma and dear Lehzen and came home at 20 minutes to 7. At ½ p.7 we dined. Stayed up till a ¼ p.10.'

There were also foreign ambassadors to see. On 19 July, she complained of having her hand kissed 3,000 times. But she relished her new role, saying it was 'the greatest pleasure to do my duty for my country and my people, and no fatigue, however great, will be burdensome to me if it is for the welfare of the nation'. When Uncle Leopold suggested that she spend more time at Claremont, she said: 'But I must see my ministers every day.'

Victoria was keen to get away from the gloom of Kensington Palace and had already decided to move to Buckingham Palace. Originally built for the Duke of Buckingham in 1703, Buckingham House had been bought by George III as a private residence for Queen Charlotte. George spent £30,000 [£3m/$3.9m in today's money] adding a library and extra rooms, but it was George IV who turned Buckingham House into a palace. In 1825, he engaged the architect John Nash, who wanted to tear the building down and start again, but the King insisted on rebuilding 'because of early associations which endear me to the spot'.

Its renovation had continued under William IV, but had yet to be completed. Despite this, Victoria wanted to move in there as soon as possible and was the first monarch to make it the principal royal residence. She insisted that the restoration be finished by 13 July 1837. The following day, she moved in, though work on the palace was still under way. She loved her new home with its large windows, mirrors and chandeliers, which filled it with light, and the rooms her mother was assigned were far from the young queen's apartment.

First impressions

The new monarch dazzled wherever she went. When she appeared in the House of Lords to close the parliamentary session, men were moved to tears, while the wife of the American ambassador said her voice was as 'sweet as a Virginia nightingale's'. She found the robe that she had to wear for the occasion enormously heavy. It was a comfort to have Lord Melbourne preceding her, carrying the Sword of State.

'He stood quite close to me on the left-hand of the Throne, and I feel always a satisfaction to have him near me on such occasions, as he is such an honest, good, kind-hearted man and is my friend, I know it. I was grieved that my dearest beloved friend Lehzen was not there, but she did not feel equal to it,' she said.

Naturally, Victoria met with her prime minister regularly and their letters contained certain intimacies and expressions of affection that the royal household's archivists decided to censor in case readers thought they were lovers. Of course, it would have been impossible for there to have been any inappropriate relationship between them. According to historian Boyd Hilton, Melbourne's private life was 'problematic': 'His marriage as William Lamb to Lady Caroline was a public disaster. He became a serial cuckold, most famously of Byron (who also consorted with his mother). It was Lady Caroline who called Byron "mad, bad and dangerous to know". Melbourne then had to endure their dirty linen being washed in public in Caroline's kiss-and-tell novel *Glenarvon*.'

Lady Caroline Lamb had died in 1828. That same year Lord Branden accused Melbourne of 'criminal conversation' with his wife, though the case was dismissed when key witnesses failed to turn up in court and Lord Branden was rewarded with a handsome bribe. In his will, Branden left just one shilling (5p) to his '*très infame et vicieuse épouse dont l'infidélité à mon égard est le moindre des crimes*' ('infamous and vicious wife whose infidelity in my view was the least of the crimes') as he referred to his wife. Meanwhile, Lady Branden received an annuity from Melbourne, though he had made it plain that the affair was over: 'I will not form a permanent connection with you,' he wrote. 'I have no present intention of ever marrying again.'

Society scandal

In 1836, Melbourne was involved in another sex scandal. The husband of a close friend, society beauty and author Caroline Norton, who Melbourne saw every day for hours at a time, accused him of adultery with his wife and demanded £10,000 [worth £1m/$1.3 in today's prices] in damages. In court Melbourne was vindicated, but he stopped seeing Mrs Norton who *The Times* described as 'imprudent, indiscreet, and undignified', while Melbourne was condemned for wasting his time with such 'contemptible and unnecessary frivolities'. He bore this stoically, as he did the death of his son later that year.

Hilton concluded: 'If his air of imperturbability was an act, it fooled young Queen Victoria, with whom he developed a close and protective relationship, he avuncular and she coquettish.'

While she could not entertain Melbourne, Victoria was happy to defy convention in other ways. On 14 November 1837, she knighted the banker and philanthropist Moses Montefiore, the first Jewish knight in English history. She would only allow men to withdraw to another room for a drink after dinner for 15 minutes and she would remain standing in her drawing room until they returned. And when Melbourne told her that it would be more proper to go to a review in Hyde Park in a carriage, she insisted instead on going on horseback. She had not ridden for two years as her mother had always insisted that Conroy accompany her. Reviewing the troops mounted in Windsor Great Park, she said: 'I felt for the first time like a man, as if I could fight myself as the head of my troops.'

She wrote to Feodora: 'Everybody says that I am quite another person since I came to the throne. I look and am so very well, I have such a pleasant life; just the sort of life I like.'

As queen, she was coming into her own.

Chapter Four

REGINAMANIA

After over a century of dissolute and disreputable kings, the new queen was loved by the country. In January 1838, the *Spectator* spoke of 'Reginamania'. Huge crowds turned out when she rode in a carriage to attend a banquet held by the Lord Mayor of London at the Guildhall. She wrote: 'Throughout my progress to the City, I met with the most gratifying, affectionate, hearty and brilliant reception from the greatest concourse of people I ever witnessed; the streets being immensely crowded as were also the windows, houses, churches, balconies, everywhere... I cannot say how gratified, and how touched I am by the very brilliant, affectionate, cordial, enthusiastic and unanimous reception I met with in this the greatest Metropolis in the World; there was not a discontented look, not a sign of displeasure – all loyalty, affection and loud greeting from the immense multitude I passed through; and no disorder whatever. I feel deeply grateful for this display of affection and unfeigned loyalty and attachment from my good people. It is much more than I deserve, and I shall do my utmost to render myself worthy of all this love and affection.'

Feodora reminded her: 'You have it in your power to make thousands happy.'

Her mother had wanted Conroy to go to the banquet, telling her daughter: 'The Queen should forget what displeased the

Princess. Recollect I have the greatest regard for Sir John, I cannot forget what he has done for me and for you, although he had the misfortune to displease you.'

As queen, Victoria began to pay off her father's debts. She increased her mother's allowance, though the Duchess continued to overspend and Victoria complained to Melbourne about the dunning letters she received. However, Wellington persuaded Conroy to resign from the Duchess of Kent's household and go abroad for a time. When he returned, he moved to the countryside where he became a gentleman farmer, specializing in pig breeding.

Victoria was kind to staff and generous to distant members of the family. Politician and diarist Thomas Creevey revealed that, from her own private funds, she was paying pensions to William IV's illegitimate children, the FitzClarences, who her mother held in contempt. Creevey also mentioned that Victoria gobbled her food and showed unattractive gums when she laughed, but she 'blushes and laughs every instant in so natural a way as to disarm anybody. Her voice is perfect, and so is the expression of her face, when she means to say or do a pretty thing.'

The coronation

At four o'clock in the morning of 28 June 1838, Victoria was awoken by guns firing a salute in Hyde Park. Before she got up the park was full of people and bands. It was the day of the coronation. 'It was a fine day; and the crowds of people exceeded what I have ever seen; many as there were, the day I went to the City, it was nothing – nothing to the multitudes, the millions of my loyal subjects who were assembled in every spot to witness the Procession,' she wrote. 'Their good-humour and excessive loyalty was beyond everything, and I really cannot say how proud I feel to be the Queen of such a Nation.'

Her coach took her up Constitution Hill, then along Piccadilly, St James's and Pall Mall to Trafalgar Square. In Whitehall, the crowds were so dense, she was afraid that people would be crushed in the throng. At one point the procession was halted by weight of numbers and the police had to clear the way with their truncheons.

Victoria arrived at Westminster Abbey soon after 11.30 where her eight train-bearers awaited, along with the newly made Imperial State Crown which cost £112,760 [£11.3 million, or $15m, today].

'My excellent Lord Melbourne who stood very close to me throughout the whole ceremony, was completely overcome at this moment, and very much affected; he gave me such a kind, and I may say, fatherly look… After the Homage was concluded, I left the Throne, took off my Crown and received the Sacrament; I then put on my Crown again, and re-ascended the Throne, leaning on Lord Melbourne's arm; at the commencement of the Anthem.'

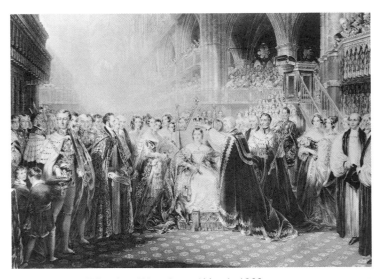

The coronation of Victoria at Westminster Abbey in 1838.

Despite the grandeur of the ceremony, there were elements of farce. Melbourne, the newly elected MP Benjamin Disraeli observed, 'looked awkward and uncouth with his coronet cocked over his nose and his robes under his feet, holding the Sword of State like a butcher'. He had an upset stomach and had dosed himself heavily with laudanum and brandy beforehand, while the archbishop had failed to rehearse and muffed his lines.

The peers queued up for the traditional kiss on the cheek. Appalled at the prospect of 600 old men nuzzling her face, she insisted that the kiss should be on the hand. Climbing the steps for the obeisance, Lord Rolle got tangled in his robe, fell over and rolled down the steps to the gasps of the congregation. The Bishop of Bath and Wells skipped a page of the order of ceremony, bringing the proceedings to a premature end.

While again the coronation was a very public spectacle, for Victoria there was also a very personal dimension: 'There was another most dear Being present at this ceremony, in the box immediately above the Royal Box, and who witnessed all,' she noted. 'It was my dearly beloved angelic Lehzen, whose eyes I caught when on the Throne, and we exchanged smiles.'

The Queen took a brief interlude in the Confessor's Chapel, where sandwiches were laid out on the altar and Melbourne seized the opportunity to down a full glass of communion wine. The ceremony was over by 4.30 p.m. Unfortunately, the ruby coronation ring had been jammed on the wrong finger and Victoria had to soak her hand in a bowl of iced water for half an hour before she could get it off. Outside the abbey, a constable had to grapple with a Captain Thomas Flowers of the Thirteenth Light Dragoons who wanted to get in to ask Victoria to marry him. He was later declared insane, the fate of a handful of others who also tried to stalk her.

'I re-entered my carriage, the Crown on my head, and Sceptre and Orb in my hand, and we proceeded the same way as we came – the crowds if possible having increased. The enthusiasm, affection and loyalty was really touching, and I shall ever remember this day as the proudest of my life.'

She got home a little after six – 'really not feeling tired'. They dined at eight.

'Lord Melbourne came up to me and said: "I must congratulate you on this most brilliant day," and that it had gone off so well… He asked kindly if I was tired; said the Sword he carried (the 1st, the Sword of State) was excessively heavy. I said that the Crown hurt me a good deal… After dinner Lord Melbourne and I spoke of the numbers of Peers at the Coronation; which, Lord Melbourne said, with the tears in his eyes, was unprecedented.'

She was thrilled when he told her that she had performed beautifully – 'every part of it, with so much taste'. He sat near her the whole evening and Feodora, who had accompanied Victoria throughout the day, stayed to see the fireworks.

The people's day out
'But we must not omit a word on the holiday of the common people, after noticing this holiday of princes,' Charles Dickens wrote in the *Examiner*. 'In the refreshment booths, of which there was a goodly show, were piled, in high and long array, butts of porter and barrels of ale, with sturdy rounds of beef and goodly hams in most bountiful abundance. There were whole streets of signs – Victoria Taverns and Coronation Taverns out of number; as many Queen's Arms as would have furnished forth an Amazonian Briareus; with patriotic emblems so complex and ingenious, that the staunchest patriot would have been at a loss to unravel their meaning.'

Victoria was a great fan of Dickens. It was one issue where she fell out with Melbourne, who was not interested in the poor. The coronation had been rather too much for him. Afterwards he took to his bed for a week, sending a note saying he was suffering from gout.

'This is most provoking and vexatious and makes me quite cross; for I'm so spoilt and accustomed to see this kind and I may venture to say even dear friend (as I look up to him with a filial confidence and affection) every day, that I'm quite annoyed and put out when my agreeable daily visit does not take place,' Victoria wrote in her journal. 'Nevertheless, I ought not to be selfish, and I must say I am glad this gout has come out; and I'm certain all that weakness and ailing he has had about him for some weeks was this gout, which he could not throw out. But I'm quite vexed and unhappy he should be again suffering; he is too good ever to suffer. And I've a Council today which must take place without him; and there I must be, as it were, with strangers and without the person who makes me feel safe and comfortable; for when Lehzen cannot be with me, I feel he replaces her; but I'm childish – though these feelings are very natural.'

Clearly, she had a deep affection for him. She wrote to him, telling him that she had cancelled the meeting of the Privy Council on his account. She missed him. Then on 4 September 1838, after a long conversation with Lord Melbourne about literature and the theatre, she wrote in her journal: 'How fond I am of this truly amiable man… I love him like a father.'

The cricketer and clerk to the Privy Council, Charles Greville, thought that Victoria's feelings for Lord Melbourne were sexual 'although, she did not know it'. Rumours abounded because they spent so much time together – eating, talking, riding and playing chess. Lady Grey wrote to Thomas Creevey: 'I hope you are amused at the report of Lord Melbourne being likely to marry the Queen. For my part I have no objection.'

Whatever Victoria's feelings were, Melbourne was busy elsewhere. Mrs Norton noted that her successor was Lady Stanhope. There were other women in his life, though he and Mrs Norton were later reconciled. On 28 August 1839, Victoria complained he was 'very inconsistent, despising and abusing women, and yet always making too much of them'. Again, on 5 December 1839, she said: 'He is always abusing the ladies and yet always running after them.'

On the other hand, Melbourne had a prudish side. He advised that his friend, Lady Holland, a divorcee, should not be presented at Court, that Victoria should not waltz and her Maids of Honour were not to walk on the terrace at Windsor Castle unchaperoned. That a man with Melbourne's reputation should be so concerned with propriety greatly amused London society. Victoria also grew jealous when Melbourne preferred to spend his evenings at a popular salon in Holland House, even asking him whether Lady Holland was prettier than she was.

Chapter Five

THE BEDCHAMBER CRISIS

When Melbourne won the first election of her reign in 1837, Victoria clapped her hands in delight. She was a committed Whig and consulted him on everything – including her looks. She feared that she was getting overweight. He remarked that the best figure for a woman was 'full with a fine bust'.

'Told him of my having carried my point about Ma's not coming into my room without previously asking, &c.; that she had been rather angry at 1st; that I was obliged sometimes to remind her of who I was; Lord M. said: "Quite right but that it was disagreeable doing so."' Her mother also complained about Victoria drinking wine, which Melbourne had recommended over the beer she preferred if she wanted to stay slim.

Victoria's close association with Melbourne and the Whig cause would soon have consequences. Lady Flora Hastings, one of the Duchess of Kent's ladies-in-waiting, came from a prominent Tory family, but Victoria suspected that she was a spy for Conroy and had little time for her. Lady Flora had spent the Christmas of 1838 with her mother in Scotland and returned in a coach with Conroy in January 1839 without a chaperone. Complaining of pains in the stomach on the journey, on her arrival she consulted the physician of the royal household, Sir James Clark, who treated her with rhubarb and camphor. Then her stomach started to swell and Lehzen and others began to suspect she was pregnant.

There were other reasons to suspect that there was something between Conroy and Lady Flora. Victoria told Melbourne that her mother disliked and was afraid of Lady Flora; '"In fact, she is jealous of her,"' said Lord M., looking sharply, as if he knew more than he liked to say; ("which God knows! I do about Flo, and which others will know too by and by"). She tells him everything the Duchess does, he said.'

Three days later they were talking of Conroy again when Melbourne, who should have known about these things, said: 'What an amazing scape of a man he must have been to have kept three ladies at once in good humour.' In her journal, Victoria added that she 'believed him capable of every villainy'.

By 2 February, Victoria was certain. She wrote: 'We have no doubt that she is – to use plain words – with child! …the horrid cause of all this is the Monster and Demon Incarnate, whose name I forbear to mention, but which is the 1st word of the 2nd line of this page,' which was, of course, 'Conroy'.

It is hard to think of a greater disgrace that could be levelled then at an unmarried, aristocratic woman and her family. Tongues began to wag, in the Court and in the newspapers. The potential for scandal was enormous. The question was, what to do about it? Sir James Clark first needed to examine Lady Flora. But doing this over her dress failed to produce a satisfactory diagnosis, though he remained suspicious. When he suggested repeating the process with her stays removed, Lady Flora declined.

Next, a senior lady of the bedchamber, Lady Emma Portman, suggested that Clark inform Lady Flora of the Court's suspicions. Two weeks later, Clark went to see her to tell her that because of her appearance the Queen's ladies were convinced that she must be 'privately married, or at least ought to be so'. Lady Flora denied it. He then said she must see a second physician. She refused.

The Duchess of Kent was informed. She was horrified and it was agreed that Lady Flora should not appear at Court again until her innocence was established. The following day Lady Flora accepted that she had no choice but to undergo another examination to disprove the allegation. Sir Charles Clarke, a specialist in women's diseases, was in Court at the time. He, Sir James Clark and Lady Portman went to see Lady Flora. With her maid as a reluctant witness, they gave her an intimate examination. Afterwards, Lady Flora wrote to her uncle, Hamilton Fitzgerald, saying: 'I have the satisfaction of possessing a certificate signed by my accuser, Sir James Clark, and also by Sir Charles Clarke, stating, as strongly as language can state it, that there are no grounds for believing pregnancy does exist, or ever existed.'

She concluded the letter saying: 'Goodbye, my dear uncle, I blush to send you so revolting a letter, but I wish you to know the truth, the whole truth, and nothing but the truth – and you are welcome to tell it left and right.'

Even then, Clarke had some misgivings, saying, 'Though she is a virgin still that it might be possible and one could not tell if such thing could happen. That there is an enlargement in the womb like a child.'

Terrible blunder

Nevertheless, Victoria realized the magnitude of her blunder. She wrote to Lady Flora apologizing and saying that she would visit her that evening if Flora wished. Victoria also said that she hoped Flora would stay on at the palace long enough to convince everyone of her innocence.

Lady Flora accepted the apology, but told the Queen: 'I must

respectfully observe, madam, I am the first, and I trust I shall be
the last, Hastings ever so treated by their sovereign. I was treated
as if guilty without a trial.'

The affair increased the acrimony between the Queen and her
mother, who sacked Sir James Clark though Victoria did not.
Fuelled by Conroy's ire, the Tories used Victoria's treatment of
her lady of the bedchamber to attack Melbourne's government,
whose advice to the Queen was called into question. At one point,
he had suggested that getting Lady Flora married off might spike
the gossip: 'This made me laugh excessively, for I said Lady F. had
neither riches or beauty or anything,' Victoria wrote.

From then on, Flora's personal agony and the damage to the
Queen filled the partisan newspapers. It became Whig (for the
Queen) against Tory (for Flora). It was dramatic – and scurrilous; it
was openly alleged that Victoria was responsible for the calumny.
Third parties were used to send private letters anonymously to
the press.

Flora's uncle, Hamilton Fitzgerald, wrote to *The Examiner*,
telling them of the ordeal his niece had undergone and quoting
widely from her letter to him. In his letter, published on 24
March, Fitzgerald said that he 'demanded and obtained from Lord
Melbourne, a distinct disavowal of his participation in the affair…

'Lady Flora is convinced that the Queen was surprised into the
order which was given, and that her majesty did not understand
what she was betrayed into; for ever since the horrid event, her
majesty has showed her regret by the most gracious kindness to
Lady Flora, and expressed it warmly, with "tears in her eyes". The
Duchess of Kent's conduct was perfect: "A mother could not have
been kinder."'

While Victoria extended her compassion to Lady Flora, she
had little time for the rest of the Hastings family, who, after all,

were Tories. In response, the Dowager Marchioness published all her correspondence with Lord Melbourne in the *Morning Post*, a Tory newspaper. The Hastings correspondence caused a media maelstrom. Victoria was outraged and said the editor should be hanged, along with the whole of the Hastings family.

It is hard to overestimate the interest that this story garnered among the general public, fuelled by articles in the newspapers and periodicals of the time. The 19th century was witnessing the arrival of the mass media: high-volume illustrated newspapers and periodicals desperate for readers. From the start, royalty had been an essential subject with which to fill their pages. Victoria's arrival as queen after years of rather dull and badly behaved kings was manna from heaven for the editors and writers who filled their pages with her. For the first two years of her reign, they had been kind to the new monarch, although they were consistent in their descriptions of her youth and inexperience. However, she was not immune from criticism, perhaps because they were not sure what to make of her, firstly as a woman – after all they had no experience of a queen since the previous female queen regnant was Elizabeth I – and secondly because she was unmarried! But the Hastings Scandal, as it was referred to, marked the first instance of actual disapproval.

Aftermath of the scandal

In early May, the government was defeated in the House of Lords by five votes when Radicals and Tories (both of whom Victoria detested) voted against a bill to suspend the constitution of Jamaica. The bill removed political power from plantation owners who were resisting measures associated with the abolition of slavery.

Such a narrow margin of victory raised the prospect that the Commons might table a vote of confidence. This terrified the Queen, who could not bear the idea of losing Melbourne: 'I am but a poor helpless girl, who clings to him for support and protection,' she wrote, 'and the thought of ALL, ALL my happiness being possibly at stake, so completely overcame me, that I burst into tears, and remained crying for some time.'

As it was, the vote of confidence was carried, but the scandal would not go away.

Early in May, Melbourne's government found itself in trouble again over the Jamaica Bill. On 7 May, Lord John Russell told the weeping Queen that Melbourne must resign. 'The state of agony, grief and despair into which this placed me, may be easier imagined than described!' she wrote. 'All, all my happiness gone!'

When he visited her at midday, she grasped both his hands and sobbed: 'You will not forsake me.' Then she said: 'I want to speak to you on a subject I've never spoken to you before of – I want to speak to you of Sir John Conroy.'

With tears in his eyes, Melbourne held up his hand and said: 'Stop, Ma'am, never speak to me of this man.'

She clung on to his hands to prevent him leaving. He declined three invitations to dinner, saying that it would be inappropriate in the circumstances. After he had gone, Victoria was so distraught at his loss that she wondered whether she might go riding in the park the following day, where she might meet him by accident.

Her duty now was to invite a Tory to form a government. The Duke of Wellington declined because he was too old. He was now deaf and had little contact with the House of Commons, though he agreed to be foreign secretary. Instead, she would have to ask Sir Robert Peel to be prime minister. However, as his Tory Party did not have a decisive measure of support in the Commons, he asked that the Queen show her support by replacing some of her ladies-in-waiting who were married or related to prominent Whigs for others who had more obvious Tory connections – a practice that was common but not enshrined in law. 'I replied that I never would consent, and I never saw a man so frightened,' said Victoria.

Peel went away to consult various officers of state and returned to ask again about the ladies. 'I said I could not give up any of my Ladies, and never had imagined such a thing; he asked if I meant to retain all; all, I said. "The Mistress of the Robes and the Ladies of the Bedchamber?" he asked. I replied all.'

Victoria said that she never talked politics with them. Besides, many of them were related to prominent Tories. When she could not be budged, Peel told her that if she would not remove some of her ladies, he would not be able to form a government. He resigned the following day. Lord Melbourne would have to continue, though he feared that there may have to be a general election that might put him in an even worse position in the House of Commons.

In the evening there was a state ball for Tsarevich Alexander, a grand duke and son of Tsar Nicholas I, where Victoria and Melbourne talked – 'Peel and the Duke of Wellington came by looking very much put out.' After Lord Melbourne left, she spent the rest of the evening dancing, showing special favour to the Tsarevich.

'I really am quite in love with the Grand Duke,' she said. 'He is a dear, delightful young man.'

When she heard that Melbourne had been hissed as he left the palace, she was furious, saying, 'Tories are capable of every villainy.'

Victoria's confession

Sixty years later, though, she admitted that she had mishandled what the newspapers dubbed the 'Bedchamber Crisis': 'Yes, I was very hot about it and so were my Ladies,' she told her private secretary, Sir Arthur Bigge, 'as I had been so brought up under Lord Melbourne; but I was very young, only twenty, and never should have acted so again. Yes, it was a mistake.'

Worse was to come. By April it was clear that Lady Flora was seriously ill, though Victoria dismissed her condition as a 'bilious attack'. On 30 May 1839, Victoria attended the races at Ascot where, she said, she was 'uncommonly well received'. According to other accounts though, when she arrived in her open-topped coach, she was hissed at by two Tory women, Lady Sarah Ingestre and the Duchess of Montrose. And when she walked out on to the royal balcony, someone shouted out: 'Mrs Melbourne!' But when Lady Flora turned up, she was loudly cheered.

Convinced that Flora was going to die, the Duchess of Kent tried repeatedly to get Victoria to speak or write to her. She finally got around to visiting Lady Flora on 27 June. 'I found poor Lady Flora stretched on a couch looking as thin as anybody can be who is still alive,' Victoria wrote, 'literally a skeleton, but the body very much swollen like a person who is with child; a searching look in her eyes, a look rather like a person who is dying.'

As Victoria left, Flora grasped her hand and said: 'I shall not see you again.'

Melbourne, who was waiting outside, admonished Victoria, saying: 'You remained a very short time.'

Lady Flora died a little after 2 a.m. on 5 July. Lehzen brought the news. A post-mortem revealed that she had an advanced cancerous tumour of the liver. The report also confirmed that 'the uterus and its appendages presented the usual appearances of the healthy virgin state'.

After that, Victoria and Melbourne were hissed at in public. Men showed their disrespect by not removing their hats when the Queen's carriage came past. When Sir Charles Napier proposed the loyal toast at a dinner in Nottingham, none of the other diners would join him.

Lady Flora's coffin was carried out of the palace at four o'clock in the morning. Even so, a large crowd had gathered to witness the cortège. A royal carriage took it to a wharf in Blackwall, from where it was to be shipped back to Scotland. As they neared the wharf, stones were thrown at the carriage. 'There's the victim, but where's the murderer?' shouted one man. 'What's the good of her gilded trumpery after she had killed her?' yelled another.

Flora's death put the scandal of her treatment by Victoria back in the newspapers. Lord Hastings gave the press new material, including the first prescription Sir James Clark had given her. Clark tried to defend himself, while *The Lancet* called him 'at best no better than a go-between'. In a pamphlet called *The Court Doctor Dissected* another doctor listed at least ten other complaints that could cause a swelling of the abdomen resembling pregnancy.

Victoria even became snappy with Lord Melbourne: 'I can't think what possessed me,' she confided, 'for I love this dear excellent man who is kindness and forbearance itself, most dearly.'

Chapter Six

THE ADORATION OF ALBERT

During the Bedchamber Crisis, Lord Melbourne mentioned the 'shocking alternative' of Victoria getting married to avoid the obsessive machinations of her mother to be her guardian and to improve her standing with the public. Uncle Leopold was urging her to marry her cousin Albert, though Melbourne pointed out that the Coburgs were not popular abroad – the Russians hated them. Albert was three months younger than her and she would prefer someone older.

'We enumerated the various Princes, of which not one, I said, would do. For myself, I said, at present my feeling was quite against ever marrying,' she wrote. However, if she were to marry, she thought that Albert might just be the right person.

'I don't think a foreigner would be popular,' warned Melbourne. But Victoria observed that by marrying a subject, you were making yourself so much their equal, and it brought you into contact with their whole family.

There were even rumours in the American press that President Martin van Buren, a widower and, at 54, the same age as Lord Melbourne, 'thinks seriously about making an offer'. The Boston *Daily Advertiser* said there was 'no reason why he should not offer, or why he may not stand as good a chance as the namby-pamby princes and kinglings of Europe.'

Victoria was not keen and expressed her doubts to Melbourne: 'I said why need I marry at all for three or four years? Did he see the necessity?' she wrote in her journal. 'I dreaded the thought of marrying; that I was so accustomed to have my own way.'

The following day, they discussed the possibility of her cousins Ernest and Albert coming over to England again: 'My having no great wish to see Albert, as the whole subject was an odious one,' Victoria wrote. 'I said I wished if possible never to marry.'

On 15 July 1839, she wrote to Leopold on 'the subject of my cousins' visit, which I am desirous should not transpire'. Although Victoria and Albert had written to each other, 'there is no engagement between us'.

The visit was planned for October and on 30 September Victoria received a letter from Albert saying they could not set off before the 6th. She noted that he and Ernest did not seem too keen to come, which shocked her. She had expected them, at least, to be keen.

The Albert effect

They arrived on 10 October after a rough crossing. When they reached Windsor, Victoria was standing at the top of the stairs. 'It was with some emotion that I beheld Albert – who is beautiful,' she said.

That evening, she asked Melbourne whether he thought Albert liked her.

'Oh! yes,' said Lord Melbourne, 'it struck me at once.'

They stayed up until 11.30 p.m.

The next morning Ernest and Albert came to her room.

'Albert really is quite charming, and so excessively handsome, such beautiful blue eyes, an exquisite nose, and such a pretty mouth, with delicate mustachios, and slight but very slight whiskers; a beautiful figure, broad in the shoulders and a fine waist. My heart is quite going,' she said.

It was not uncommon for Victoria to find men 'excessively handsome'. Those that measured up included the late Duke of Richmond and Monsieur de Melcy – 'I thought him very handsome last year, but he has so much *embelli*, since then. He has beautiful small features, very fine dark eyes, dark hair, moustaches and whiskers.' Women could be 'excessively handsome' too. One such was a Miss Lindley, a professional singer and the first wife of Charles Sheridan, father of Brinsley Sheridan.

After dinner, she talked to Lord Melbourne about his drinking liqueur, which she said was bad for him. Then she danced five quadrilles – two with 'dearest Albert, who dances so beautifully'. She enjoyed watching him dance too.

'It is quite a pleasure to look at Albert when he gallops and valses; he does it so beautifully, holds himself so well, with that beautiful figure of his,' she noted. 'I have to keep a tight hold on my heart.'

On 13 October, Victoria told Melbourne that she had changed her opinion on marriage. Melbourne advised her to think about it for another week, though he conceded that Albert was 'certainly a very fine young man, very good looking'. But the next day, she told Melbourne that she had made up her mind. With tears in his eyes, Melbourne said: 'I think it will be very well received... and I'm very glad of it. I think it is a very good thing.'

Victoria thanked him for being 'so fatherly about all this'.

Putting the question

By convention, as monarch, she had to propose. As she did not have a father, or a mother she could confide in, she was on her own. The following day she sent for Albert: 'I said to him, that I thought he must be aware why I wished them to come here,' she wrote, 'and that it would make me too happy if he would consent to what I wished (to marry me); we embraced each other over and over again, and he was so kind, so affectionate; oh! to feel I was, and am, loved by such an Angel as Albert, was too great a delight to describe! he is perfection; perfection in every way – in beauty – in everything! I told him I was quite unworthy of him and kissed his dear hand – he said he would be very happy, *das Leben mit dir zu bringen* (to spend life with you), and was so kind, and seemed so happy, that I really felt it was the happiest brightest moment in my life, which made up for all that I had suffered and endured. Oh! how I adore and love him, I cannot say! How I will strive to make him feel as little as possible the great sacrifice he has made; I told him it was a great sacrifice – which he wouldn't allow.'

They agreed to marry the following February, but for the moment their plans were to be kept secret – though his father, Uncle Leopold and Stockmar could be let in on the secret. He would send a message to Coburg by courier. The circle in on the secret soon widened. Albert summoned Ernest who congratulated them. After talking for a while, Victoria sent Albert off with a kiss. He went to tell Lehzen while she fired off a letter to Leopold. It read: 'This letter will, I am sure, give you pleasure, for you have always shown and taken so warm an interest in all that concerns me. My mind is quite made up – and I told Albert this morning of it; the warm affection he showed me on learning this gave me great pleasure. He seems perfection, and I think that I have the prospect of very great happiness before me. I love him more than I can say, and shall do everything in my power to render this sacrifice (for sacrifice in my opinion it is) as small as I can. He seems to have great tact – a very necessary thing in his position. These last few days have passed like a dream to me, and I am so much bewildered by it all that I know hardly how to write; but I do feel very, very happy.'

She explained that her feelings had changed since spring, when she could not think of marrying for three or four years – 'seeing Albert has changed all this,' she said. She was clear that parliament had no say in the matter and she would convene the Privy Council to announce her intentions.

'Oh! dear Uncle, I do feel so happy! I do so adore Albert,' she concluded.

Only her mother was not told about the marriage until a few days before Albert's departure on 14 November. She pretended to be happy about it, though she knew her daughter's marriage meant that she would be banished from the royal household.

Meanwhile, Albert was often overwhelmed by Victoria's passion. The night before he left, she wrote in her diary: 'I said to Albert we should be very very intimate together, and that he might come in and out when he pleased.'

He reprimanded her, saying she should not ask such things. But she was insistent.

'Oh! how happy shall I be, to be very very intimate with him!' she wrote.

Such sweet sorrow

Before he left the following day, they spent time alone kissing and she gave him one final kiss at the top of the staircase before he got in his carriage and drove off.

'I cried much, felt wretched, yet happy to think we should meet so soon again!' she wrote in her journal. 'Oh! how I love him, how intensely, how devotedly, how ardently!'

Victoria told Melbourne that love had made her quite stupid. Her head had been turned by his athletic physique – particularly when he wore tight white pantaloons 'with nothing under them'. However, he was a serious man. She touched on his dislike of the Russians, the French and Jews. Melbourne dismissed Albert's anti-Semitism as typically German. This was odd because his mother, Princess Louise, had been dismissed from the court of Saxe-Coburg-Gotha for having an affair with the Jewish chamberlain, the Baron von Mayern, a cultivated, intelligent, musical man. Both Albert's stupid, lecherous, drunken and nominal father, Duke Ernest of Saxe-Coburg, and his brother Ernest had hereditary syphilis, but there is no evidence of any trace of this in Albert who, like the Baron von Mayern, was intelligent, musical and cultivated.

Duke Ernest himself suspected that Albert's real father was his childhood friend Alexander Graf zu Solms, who was sent into exile. It has also been suggested that his father was Victoria's Uncle Leopold who took such a close interest in his career. Seven months after she was divorced, Princess Louise married Alexander von Hanstein who was named in the divorce proceedings as the co-respondent. She died of uterine cancer in Paris in 1831. The following year, Duke Ernest married his niece Duchess Marie of Württemberg, the daughter of his sister Antoinette. This marriage made Marie both Prince Albert's first cousin and his stepmother.

Victoria's declaration to the Privy Council of her intention to marry made on 23 November was again written by Melbourne. It said: 'I have caused you to be summoned at the present time, in order that I may acquaint you with my resolution in a matter which deeply concerns the welfare of my people, and the happiness of my future life. It is my intention to ally myself in marriage with the Prince Albert of Saxe-Coburg and Gotha. Deeply impressed with the solemnity of the engagement which I am about to contract, I have not come to this decision without mature consideration, nor without feeling a strong assurance that, with the blessing of Almighty God, it will at once secure my domestic felicity and serve the interests of my country. I have thought fit to make this resolution known to you at the earliest period, in order that you may be fully apprised of a matter so highly important to me and to my kingdom, and which I persuade myself will be most acceptable to all my loving subjects.'

Melbourne was in tears again. Victoria wanted to send the declaration to Albert. Fortunately, Melbourne had another copy in his pocket.

Generally, the announcement was accepted favourably. However, the *Spectator* pointed out that Albert was 'a gilded puppet, who can perform no action becoming an elevated birth and exalted station; who can follow no pursuit worthy of a warrior or a statesman; whose entire importance is reflected, and who can avow no opinion (except, perhaps, on an article of dress, a piece of furniture, or a horse), even though the fate and character of his wife be at stake, without violating the constitution of the country that has adopted him! Happiness may, nevertheless, be the fate of the illustrious pair, and there can be no exaggeration in saying that the best wishes of the nation for their felicity will attend the union. But to domestic happiness the public can contribute little beyond good wishes.'

Cold fish

This did nothing to dampen his ardour. On 30 November, Albert, who admitted to being a cold fish, wrote: 'Dearly beloved Victoria – I long to talk to you; otherwise the separation is too painful. Your dear picture stands on my table in front of me, and I can hardly take my eyes off it… What a delight it must be to walk through the whole of my life, with its joys and sorrows, with you at my side!… Love of you fills my whole heart… Think sometimes with love of your Albert, whose heart beats truly and honourably for you, and whose dearest wish is that your love may continue… I kiss you a thousand times. May Heaven bless you.'

The following January Lord John Russell proposed that Prince Albert be given an allowance of £50,000 [£5 million in today's money or $6.8m]. The Tories, under Peel, voted to cut it to £30,000 [£3 million in today's money or $3.9m].

'As long as I live, I'll never forgive these infernal scoundrels, with Peel at their head, for this act of personal spite!' Victoria wrote.

Then there was the question of precedence – where, exactly, he would stand in the pecking order. In official processions Albert would follow directly behind her. Her uncles and the Tories objected.

'Poor dear Albert, how cruelly are they ill-using that dearest Angel! Monsters! You Tories shall be punished. Revenge, revenge!' she wrote. This time she blamed the Duke of Wellington. Melbourne had to bend over backwards to get him an invitation to the wedding. Nevertheless, the bill for Albert's naturalization finally went through without any mention of precedence.

More disappointment was in store for Albert. He wrote to Victoria suggesting that their honeymoon be longer than the two or three days at Windsor she had planned. She replied: 'You forget, my dearest Love, that I am Sovereign, and that business can stop and wait for nothing. Parliament is sitting, and something occurs almost every day, for which I may be required, and it is quite impossible for me to be away from London; therefore, two or three days is already a long time to be absent.'

Albert was also annoyed that Victoria and Melbourne were appointing his staff and worried that they might all be Whigs: 'If I am really to keep myself free from all parties, my people must not belong exclusively to one side,' he wrote. 'Above all do I wish that they should be well educated men of high character.'

One of his attendants was to be Melbourne's own private secretary George Anson.

'I know personally nothing of Mr George Anson, except that I have seen him dance a quadrille,' he complained. But Victoria was adamant.

'I have exhausted all my arguments on that point, and written myself nearly blind to make you understand how distasteful it all is to me,' Albert wrote. 'It was the first and only request with which I appealed to your love, and I do not wish to make a second; but I declare calmly that I will not take Mr Anson nor anybody now.'

Nevertheless, Anson was appointed as Albert's private secretary. The only concession made was that he resigned from Melbourne's staff. Next, Victoria and Melbourne decided to appoint someone to control the Prince's finances.

'As the Queen's husband,' he wrote just a month before the wedding, 'I shall be in a dependent position, more dependent than any other husband, in my domestic circumstances. My private fortune is all that remains to me to dispose of. I am therefore not unfair in requesting that that which has belonged to me since I came of age nearly a year ago (and indeed belongs to any grown man) shall be left under my control.'

He reminded her that their disagreements did not mean 'failure of my love towards yourself, which nothing can shake', concluding: 'With burning love for you, I remain, your faithful, Albert.'

Albert's position

At the very least, Albert wanted a seat in the House of Lords, but Victoria wanted him to have a royal rank. Melbourne told her that making him king was out of the question. Victoria was sovereign and would remain so. Consequently, she had to lay down some ground rules. He was not to get involved in politics. They were to be seen to agree on everything. He was to support the policy pursued by her government and his staff must be generally sympathetic to the ruling party.

'I hope Lord Melbourne does not think we want to lead a life of strife and dissension instead of love and unity,' Albert countered. 'One's opinions are not to be dictated, for an opinion is the result of reflection and conviction, and you could not respect a husband who never formed an opinion till you had formed yours, and whose opinions were always the same as yours.'

When the archbishop asked Victoria if she wanted the word 'obey' removed from the wedding service, she declined. She also suggested to Melbourne that all cavalry officers should grow a thin moustache like the one sported by the young Albert, which he went along with. At Melbourne's suggestion, the service would take place in the Chapel Royal of St James's Palace, even though she disliked it. He also insisted that she invite some Tories.

Albert wanted all the bridesmaids to be the daughters of mothers seen to be virtuous, but Victoria was not so prim. She even included the daughter of Lady Jersey, one of George IV's many mistresses. Over the objections of Melbourne and her mother, Victoria insisted that Albert sleep under the same roof as her on the night before their wedding as it would make her calmer. Consequently, she slept well.

Rising at 8.45 a.m. on 10 February 1840, Victoria wrote a note to Albert, saying: 'Dearest, how are you today, and have you slept well? I have rested very well, and feel very comfortable today. What weather! I believe however, the rain will cease. Send one word when you, my most dearly beloved bridegroom, will be ready. Thy ever-faithful, VICTORIA R.'

Contemporary engraving of the wedding of Victoria and Albert.

They met briefly before Albert left for the Chapel Royal ahead of her.

For the wedding, Victoria wore a heavy white silk satin dress, trimmed with Honiton lace. It had a six-yard train edged with orange blossoms. The dress sat low on the shoulders to show off her smooth, white chest. She wore a diamond necklace and diamond earrings. A sapphire brooch given to her by Albert was pinned to her bodice. On her feet, she wore white satin slippers, attached to her ankles with ribbons. Her hair was parted in the middle and looped into low buns on either side of her head, and crowned with a wreath of orange blossoms and myrtle, as symbols of fertility.

Day of the ceremony

Despite strong winds and torrential rain, the crowds did turn out. London had been in a ferment of anticipation for weeks about the impending nuptials. No one was immune to excitement; even the pre-eminent writer of the era, Charles Dickens, joked with his friends that he, too, was a victim of it. In a letter to the poet Walter Savage Landor, he wrote: 'Society is unhinged here by Her Majesty's marriage, and I am sorry to add that I have fallen hopelessly in love with the Queen.' The controversial weekly newspaper, *The Satirist* (the *Private Eye* of its time), complained: 'We are all going stark staring mad. Nothing is heard or thought of but doves and Cupids, triumphal arches and white favours, and last, but not least, variegated lamps and general illuminations.' After a year of hissing, name-calling and savaging by the press, it seemed as if Londoners were once more in love with their queen.

She rode the short distance from Buckingham Palace to the Chapel Royal in a golden carriage, accompanied by her mother and the Duchess of Sutherland, Mistress of the Robes and the

Whigs' leading political hostess. The crowds that thronged the muddy streets were held back by police, the trees full of those in search of a better vantage point. Victoria's party had to wait briefly while Albert's procession, which included a squadron of Life Guards, entered the chapel. They then assembled in the throne room with her 12 young train-bearers dressed in white with white roses. Melbourne wore a new dress coat, which he said had been built like a 74-gun ship, and carried the Sword of State.

A flourish of trumpets announced her arrival in the Chapel. As she entered, the organ began to play. Albert stood at the altar dressed in a tightly fitting red uniform decorated with the collar and star of the Order of the Garter. Victoria was given away by her uncle, the Duke of Sussex.

'The Ceremony was very imposing, and fine and simple, and I think ought to make an everlasting impression on every one who promises at the Altar to keep what he or she promises,' said Victoria. 'Dearest Albert repeated everything very distinctly. I felt so happy when the ring was put on, and by (my precious) Albert. As soon as the Service was over, the Procession returned as it came, with the exception that my beloved Albert led me out. The applause was very great, in the Colour Court, as we came through; Lord Melbourne, good man, was very much affected during the Ceremony and at the applause.'

The only correction she wanted to make to the official account of the wedding was that it said she had cried: 'I did not shed one tear the whole time,' she said.

They returned to the throne room, where they signed the register. It was noticed that Victoria kissed her aunt, Queen Adelaide, but only shook hands with her mother, the Duchess. Victoria and Albert then returned to Buckingham Palace. They spent half an hour alone in her room before going down to the wedding breakfast,

where Lord Melbourne assured her that the ceremony had
been perfect.

'Nothing could have gone off better,' he said.

Afterwards, they changed and, at four o'clock, set off for
Windsor, where they were to dine, 'but I had such a sick headache
that I could eat nothing, and was obliged to lie down in the middle
blue room for the remainder of the evening, on the sofa...'

But nothing could spoil her happiness: '...ill or not, I never,
never spent such an evening!! My dearest dearest dear Albert sat on
a footstool by my side, and his excessive love and affection gave me
feelings of heavenly love and happiness, I never could have hoped
to have felt before! He clasped me in his arms, and we kissed each
other again and again! His beauty, his sweetness and gentleness,
really how can I ever be thankful enough to have such a Husband!

'At ½ p.10 I went and undressed and was very sick, and at 20 m.
p.10 we both went to bed; (of course in one bed), to lie by his side,
and in his arms, and on his dear bosom, and be called by names of
tenderness, I have never yet heard used to me before – was bliss
beyond belief! Oh! this was the happiest day of my life! May God
help me to do my duty as I ought and be worthy of such blessings!'

She was sure that things could only get better.

'When day dawned (for we did not sleep much) and I beheld that
beautiful angelic face by my side, it was more than I can express!
He does look so beautiful in his shirt only, with his beautiful throat
seen,' she said.

They breakfasted together.

'He had a black velvet jacket on, without any neck cloth on, and
looked more beautiful than it is possible for me to say.'

They talked, then went for a walk together. After lunch, Albert
felt unwell, but nevertheless read a funny story to her from a
German book. After dinner, they sang. Albert complained of a

weakness in his knees and they were in bed by eleven.

The following morning, she said: 'His love and gentleness is beyond everything, and to kiss that dear soft cheek, to press my lips to his, is heavenly bliss. I feel a purer more unearthly feel than I ever did. Oh! was ever woman so blessed as I am!'

Chapter Seven

MARRIED LIFE

O n the second day of their honeymoon, they sat at separate
tables in her sitting room and tried to write, but ended up
talking. Melbourne came and they chatted about her mother's
new house in Belgrave Square. That evening there was a ball.
The dancing 'put us both so in mind of our dances in the autumn,
and particularly when I pressed his hand as I used to do – he
could hardly believe, he said, we were married.'

They stayed up until 11.50 p.m. After she undressed, she
'returned to the Bedroom. where I found dearest Albert asleep
on the sofa, looking quite beautiful; I touched his cheek with my
hand, but it did not wake him, and I then woke him with a kiss. He
took me in his arms (in bed) and kissed me again and again, and
we fell asleep arm in arm, and woke so again.'

The following morning: 'My dearest Albert put on my stockings
for me. I went in and saw him shave.'

Then Melbourne arrived with bad news from China, where
the authorities were trying to restrict the import of opium, which
would lead to the first Opium War two years later. They discussed
new additions to Albert's staff and she again complained about
how little money he was given. The newly-weds danced again
that night. Then their short honeymoon was over. The following
afternoon they headed back to a London shrouded in thick fog.

Soon Albert was missing his family. Two weeks after the wedding, his father went back to Germany. After he left, Albert passed Victoria in the hall and hurried upstairs without saying a word. She followed him: 'He was much affected, & I tried my best to comfort him,' she said. 'He seemed pleased at my sympathy, but said, with truth, that I had never had a happy childhood, never had known a father, & therefore it was difficult for me to realise, what this parting & breaking with the past meant to him. But I could make up for it all! God knows how great my wish is to make this beloved Being, happy & contented, & that I will do all in my power to assure this.'

Albert's problem
Weather permitting, Victoria and Albert took walks together around the garden. Otherwise she was absorbed in Henry Hallam's *Constitutional History of England*. It had been recommended by Lord Melbourne and she read it to Albert at night. While Albert made her laugh, he was fundamentally a serious man and liked to invite leading authors and scientists to the Court. This made Victoria feel insecure as she did not feel that her education was up to their intellectual conversation. And there were other problems at home. She continued to meet Melbourne and her ministers without him.

In May, he wrote to his friend Prince William of Löwenstein: 'In my home life I am very happy and contented; but the difficulty of filling my place with proper dignity is that I am only the husband, and not the master in the house.'

Albert complained that he was prevented from discussing politics even when they were alone together.

She discussed the problem with Melbourne. 'She said it proceeded entirely from indolence,' Melbourne recorded. 'She knew it was wrong, but when she was with the Prince she preferred talking upon other subjects.'

Melbourne told her that she should try and alter this, and that there was no objection to her conversing with the Prince upon any subject she pleased.

'My impression is that the chief obstacle in Her Majesty's mind is the fear of difference of opinion, and she thinks that domestic harmony is more likely to follow from avoiding subjects likely to create difference,' Melbourne said. 'My own experience leads me to think that subjects between man and wife, even where difference is sure to ensue, are much better discussed than avoided, for the latter course is sure to beget distrust.'

Standing up to Albert

Victoria rejected all advice she was given on this subject. She continued to see her ministers alone. Albert was not allowed to see state papers and she would take no advice from him on public matters. When a box of state papers arrived with a note telling her to 'sign immediately', Albert advised her not to do so for a day or so, otherwise they may dismiss her as nothing but a clerk. She picked up a pen and signed.

Biographer Lytton Strachey said that one story, 'ill-authenticated and perhaps mythical', summed up the situation: 'When, in wrath, the Prince one day had locked himself into his room, Victoria, no less furious, knocked on the door to be admitted. "Who is there?" he asked. "The Queen of England" was the answer. He did not move, and again there was a hail of knocks. The question and the answer were repeated many times; but at last there was a pause, and then a gentler knocking. "Who is there?" came once more the relentless question. But this time the reply was different. "Your wife, Albert." And the door was immediately opened.'

Slowly Albert did manage to find a role. In 1850, he wrote to the Duke of Wellington, describing his purpose as being: 'to sink his own individual existence in that of his wife; to aim at no power by himself or for himself; to shun all ostentation; to assume no separate responsibility before the public – to make his position entirely a part of hers – to fill up every gap which, as a woman, she would naturally leave in the exercise of her regal functions – continually and anxiously to watch every part of the public business, in order to be able to advise and assist her at any moment in any of the multifarious and difficult questions brought before her, political, social, or personal – to place all his time and powers at her command "as the natural head of her family, superintendent of her household, manager of her private affairs, her sole confidential adviser in politics, and only assistant in her communications with the officers of the government, her private secretary, and permanent minister".'

Alarming incident

On 10 June 1840, Victoria – by now four months pregnant – was taking a daily outing with Albert. Their open carriage was climbing Constitution Hill when a shot rang out. The carriage halted. They looked round and saw a man on the footpath 'no more than six paces away' with a pistol in each hand. Albert squeezed her hand and told her not to be alarmed. 'I assured him I was not the least frightened, which was the case. It never entered my head, nor did it his, after the 1st shot, that it was meant for me,' she recorded.

Albert said he 'asked if the fright had not shaken her, but she laughed at the thing. I then looked again at the man, who was still standing in the same place, his arms crossed… His attitude was so affected and theatrical it quite amused me. Suddenly he again pointed his pistol and fired a second time.'

Victoria saw the man taking aim and, Albert remembered: 'stooped quickly, drawn down by me... the many people who stood round us and the man, and were at first petrified with fright on seeing what had happened, now rushed upon him.'

Albert ordered the coachman to drive on 'partly to give Victoria a little air, and partly also to show the public that we had not... lost all confidence in them'. They headed for her mother's house and told the Duchess what had happened. Returning via Regent's and Hyde Parks, they were greeted by a cheering crowd, grateful to see them safely back at the palace. Riders followed them. It was, she said, 'a triumphal procession'. Although Victoria's composure had been faultless in public, back in her room she was badly shaken. Albert put his arms round her and kissed her, praising her courage. 'My chief anxiety was lest the fright should have been injurious to Victoria in her present state, but she is quite well...' wrote Albert.

Charged with high treason, the would-be assassin Edward Oxford was found not guilty by reason of insanity and detained at Her Majesty's pleasure, though it also emerged during the trial that there was no proof that the duelling pistols he used were loaded with anything but gunpowder. Oxford was sent to the State Criminal Lunatic Asylum in Bethlem, Southwark, where he remained as a model patient for 24 years. Transferred to Broadmoor in 1864, he was found to be sane. Three years later he was released and moved to Melbourne, Australia, and told that if he ever returned to the UK he would be imprisoned for life.

Unbowed, Victoria continued to appear in public, riding in an open carriage. However, the attack had re-ignited old fears. When the police searched Oxford's lodgings, they found a note that implied his actions had been prompted by 'some communications of an important nature from Hanover'. Was her Uncle Ernest, Duke of Cumberland – now King of Hanover – trying to kill her before she produced an heir so he could seize the throne? It was noted that Oxford's pistols had the monogram 'ER' on them. Did that stand for Ernestus Rex?

Albert showed her the pistols 'which might have finished me'. But her worry was that she would be finished off like Princess Charlotte. Victoria was almost halfway through her pregnancy. Before she married, she had written in her journal that having a lot of children was 'the only thing I dread'. And when she learned that she was pregnant she said she was 'furious. It was too dreadful.'

Just a week before the incident, she had written to her grandmother, the Dowager Duchess of Saxe-Coburg and Gotha, about her pregnancy: 'It is spoiling my happiness; I have always hated the idea and I prayed God night and day for me to be left free for at least six months, but my prayers have not been answered and I am really most unhappy. I cannot understand how one can wish for such a thing, especially at the beginning of a marriage.' She told Uncle Leopold that if she was 'rewarded only by a nasty girl' she would drown it.

The impending birth

With the perils of childbirth uppermost in everyone's mind, on 2 July 1840, Melbourne told her: 'There is a subject I must mention, which is of great importance, and one of great emergency perhaps you may anticipate what I mean.'

She said she did not.

'It is about having a bill for a Regency. I did not wish to mention it before I had spoken to the Duke of Wellington. He quite agreed that there ought [to be] no Council of Regency, but that it ought to be one person, who should be the prince. The duke was very nice about it.'

Peel and the other Tory leaders had agreed and Melbourne intended to put the matter before the Cabinet once he had mentioned it to her.

Parliament approved the bill. Albert was overjoyed. 'I am to be Regent – alone – Regent, without a Council,' he wrote to his brother Ernest. 'You will understand the importance of this matter and that it gives my position here in the country a fresh significance.'

Albert was delighted when he was allowed to sit on a throne next to Victoria at the prorogation of Parliament. In September, he was made a Privy Councillor and began to receive state papers. He wrote to Baron von Stockmar, saying that he was 'extremely pleased with Victoria during the past few months. She had only twice had the sulks... Altogether she puts more confidence in me daily.'

Despite her growing belly, Victoria continued dancing, going on long walks and working hard. Albert tried to force her to rest, reading or singing to her as she lay on a sofa. But her obstetrician, Charles Locock, disapproved of her frankness when discussing her condition and that she 'goes without stays or anything that keeps her shape within bounds'. She was, he said, 'very ugly and enormously fat... more like a barrel than anything else.'

Victoria gave birth on 21 November 1840 at Buckingham Palace. Albert was with her during the 12-hour labour. She later recorded: 'We both expressed joy that the event was at hand, & I did not feel at all nervous. After a good many hours suffering, a perfect little child was born at 2 in the afternoon, but alas! a girl & not a boy, as we both had so hoped & wished for. We were, I am afraid, sadly disappointed, but yet our hearts were full of gratitude, for God having brought me safely through my ordeal, & having such a strong, healthy child. Dearest Albert hardly left me at all, & was the greatest support & comfort.'

When Victoria was told that the child was a girl, she said: 'Never mind, the next will be a prince.' She would be christened Victoria, but would be known in the household as 'Vicky'.

Victoria dismissed the romantic idea that giving birth was in any way a spiritual endeavour, saying: 'I think much more of our being like a cow or a dog at such moments; when our poor nature becomes so very animal and unecstatic.'

After the birth, Albert dashed downstairs to represent the Queen at the Privy Council for the first time. He would soon be handling her boxes. Anson remarked that the prince was, 'in fact, tho' not in name, Her Majesty's Private Secretary'.

For two weeks after Vicky's birth Victoria recuperated privately, cared for by her husband. He was content to sit by her in a darkened room, to read to her, or write for her. He alone lifted her from her bed to the sofa, and he always helped wheel her on the bed or the sofa into the next room. To do this, he would come instantly when sent for from any part of the house.

Bringing up baby

Victoria was not an attentive mother. She called babies 'nasty objects', saying even 'the prettiest are frightful'.

At first, she called Vicky 'the Child' and saw her just twice a day when she was brought to her dressing room. Every few weeks, she watched her being bathed and noted her 'big body and little limbs and that terrible frog-like action'. She did not breastfeed – a thing that filled her with a 'totally insurmountable disgust'. She thought it vulgar, unseemly for aristocratic women and incompatible with her public duties. A wet nurse was found.

In later years, she even barred her daughters from doing it and was horrified when they ignored her advice, telling them: 'It makes my hair stand on end that my daughters have turned into cows.'

However, a bond between mother and child did develop. After just three weeks, Victoria was calling the new born 'our dear little child', noting she already had pretty light brown hair: 'She gets daily prettier, & is so *éveillé* [awake] for her age,' said Victoria. 'I hope & think she will be like her beloved Father. She has large, bright, dark blue eyes, a nice little nose & mouth, a very good complexion, with a little colour in her cheeks, very unusual, for so young a Baby.'

The end of the year was tinged with tragedy when Victoria's childhood pet, her spaniel Dash, died on Christmas Eve: 'Albert told me that poor dear old "Dash", was dead, which grieved me so much,' she wrote. 'I was so fond of the poor little fellow, & he was so attached to me. I had had him since the beginning of Feb 1833.'

Dash was buried under a marble effigy at Adelaide Cottage, Windsor, with a plaque saying:

Here lies
DASH
The favourite spaniel of Her Majesty Queen Victoria
In his 10th year
His attachment was without selfishness
His playfulness without malice
His fidelity without deceit
READER
If you would be beloved and die regretted
Profit from the example of
DASH

But there was comfort on hand. On Christmas Day 1840, Victoria wrote: 'This day, last year, I was an unmarried girl, & this year I have an angelic husband, & a dear little girl 5 weeks old!'

By February 1841, she was saying: 'Went up to see the Child, Albert soon joining. Little Victoria was so dear & merry; she is quite a little toy for us & a great pet; always smiling so sweetly, when we play with her.'

Afterwards she and Albert read despatches together and played the piano.

Vicky's christening took place at Buckingham Palace on 10 February, their first wedding anniversary. To mark the event, Albert gave Victoria a brooch shaped like a cradle with a baby in it. It was, she said, 'the quaintest thing I ever saw & so pretty'.

By April 'the Child' had become 'Pussy', the pet name she would use for Vicky from then on. In May, she was noting that Pussy was getting 'more intelligent every day'.

Albert, too, was a hands-on father. Victoria wrote to Uncle Leopold telling him: 'Our young lady flourishes exceedingly… I think you would be amused to see Albert dancing her in his arms; he makes a capital nurse (which I do not, and she is much too heavy for me to carry), and she already seems to [be] happy to go to him.'

He even got Sir Edwin Landseer to paint a portrait of Albert cradling the infant to give to Victoria.

The Queen was up and around within a month. As child-rearing could be left to the servant, she quickly got back to work. However, three months after giving birth she found herself pregnant again though was far from happy about it. Later she told her daughter that childbearing was 'a complete violence to all one's feeling of propriety (which God knows receive a shock enough in marriage alone).'

Chapter Eight

ALBERT ASCENDANT

The lax security of the palace had been breached several times between 1838 and 1841 by a teenage waif named Edward Jones, the son of a tailor in Westminster. 'The Boy Jones', as the newspapers called him, had even been in the Queen's bedroom and stolen letters, a portrait and some of her underwear. Much was made of the story. After a spell in a house of correction, Jones was forced to join the Royal Navy. In 1844, on his return to London he was re-arrested in the vicinity of the palace and finally deported to Australia.

The Prince used this lack of security as an excuse to impose Teutonic discipline on the palace. Servants were punished for scams they had been working for years and their salaries were cut. He slashed budgets, using some of the money saved to introduce modern flushing water closets to Buckingham Palace. Instead of having three government departments responsible, one officer would be in charge of the administration of the palace. The gaming tables were removed from Windsor and no one would be allowed to sit down in the Queen's presence – or Albert's. Ministers had to back out of the room and Court dress was mandatory.

Dishonesty and 'sexually loose behaviour' would be punished and notices outlining a strict code of conduct were hung in the bedrooms. Victoria did not share her husband's insistence on high moral standards, but she did little to stem his fervour. She would let him be master in his own home.

The Queen, too, would be subject to Albert's strictures. Breakfast would be at nine. Then they would walk and write together. Lunch was at two. She would see Melbourne for a couple of hours in the afternoon, then she would go for a drive. Dinner was at eight and, wherever possible, it would be early to bed.

Albert was also manoeuvring in the political field. With the Whig government now foundering, he sent Anson as an emissary to Robert Peel without Victoria's consent, offering the resignations of three senior ladies-in-waiting – the Duchess of Sutherland, the Duchess of Bedford and Lady Normanby – who were married to leading Whigs. He also told Melbourne that, with the Queen pregnant again, he should be allowed to sit in on their meetings.

To preserve the dignity of the throne, Peel insisted that the Queen herself inform him that the positions were vacant. Victoria quickly realized what Albert was up to. On 9 May 1841, she recorded: 'After luncheon my kind excellent Ld Melbourne came, & remained some time. He told me that Anson had seen Peel (which I had no idea of, but which of course Albert must have known).'

Melbourne handed her a transcript of the offer Anson had made to Peel on Albert's behalf. He advised her to go along with the deal Albert had made. Later in the day, she wrote: 'Felt very low.' But she did not take umbrage, saying: 'Albert was so kind, affectionate & anxious to do anything he could for me, that I really cannot say what a comfort, blessing & support he is to me. After 5 we walked for nearly an hour in the garden.'

That night she fretted about the impending loss of Melbourne, wishing that it was just a bad dream. She cried over the loss of her ladies, particularly the Duchess of Bedford, who had not wanted to go, and grew depressed over the way Albert and Melbourne had manipulated her. She still disliked Albert taking part in politics or the affairs of the country, and was jealous if he was well received at an event.

Melbourne goes

In June, Melbourne lost a vote of confidence and parliament was dissolved. The election was won with a thumping majority by the Conservative Party – the name the Tories had now adopted. Melbourne resigned on 28 August. After his last official audience with the Queen, they said their tearful goodbyes on the terrace at Windsor.

'For four years, I have seen you daily and liked it better every day,' said Melbourne.

While Peel irritated Victoria, Albert got on well with him. They had many interests in common. With Melbourne gone, Albert became her sole adviser. Melbourne approved of his replacement, praising the Prince's 'judgment, temper and discretion'. Looking back on their relationship, Victoria had become slightly embarrassed about her youthful infatuation with Lord Melbourne, writing on 1 October 1842: 'Wrote, & looked over & corrected one of my old Journals, which do not now awake very pleasant feelings. The life I led then was so artificial & superficial, & yet I thought I was happy. Thank God! I know now what real happiness means!'

After dinner on 17 December, she and Albert talked about 'my life before I married, & after I came to the Throne, – my unbounded affective for & admiration of Ld Melbourne which I said to Albert, I hardly knew from what it arose, excepting the fact, that relying on someone & having very warm feelings Albert thinks I worked myself up to what really become at last, quite foolish.'

Victoria and Melbourne continued to exchange letters until his death in 1848.

Albert now only had one rival for the affections of the Queen – Lehzen. She sought to undermine him, thinking that he, like her, should only seek influence with the Queen on private matters and not seek a public role. Albert called her *die Blaste* – 'the hag' – in letters to his brother.

During the 1841 election, Victoria had toured the great Whig houses to show her support for Melbourne. It was the first time she had been parted from Lehzen since she was five. They exchanged letters, but Lehzen remained behind at Windsor to look after Vicky. In the autumn, the child grew ill. Albert secretly blamed Lehzen. Vicky's condition worsened after the birth of her mother's second child on 9 November 1841. Victoria wrote: 'Pussy terrified at, & not at all pleased with, her little brother.'

Victoria was a small woman, less than five feet tall, and again the birth was an ordeal. In her journal, she wrote: 'I will not say much, but my sufferings were really very severe and I doubt that I should have died but for the great comfort and support of my beloved Albert [who] was with me, during the whole time. At last at 12 m to 11 I gave birth to a fine, large boy! Oh, how happy, how grateful did I feel that Almighty Providence has so greatly blessed me and preserved me so mercifully through so many days and trials. Though tired, I felt very well once the child was there.'

Again, she was rewarded with a jewelled brooch, this one bearing the crest of their son, Albert Edward, or 'Bertie' as he became known. And again, Victoria felt nothing for the child – at first.

As Victoria slipped into post-natal depression, Lehzen came down with jaundice. Albert called her 'the Yellow Lady' and said she went around spitting venom like a she-dragon. To raise Victoria's spirits, Albert took her to Claremont in January 1842, but they were called back to Windsor when Vicky's condition took a turn for the worse.

Close call

They found the child pale and thin. The anxious parents' tempers flared and a big row ensued. Albert said that Victoria and Lehzen had neglected the child. They had as good as killed her. Victoria shot back, accusing him of trying to control everything – even the nursery. She said he was jealous of her affection for her treasured Lehzen and she was sorry she had ever married him.

Telling himself 'I must have patience', Albert left the room, only to write to her, saying: 'Doctor Clark has mismanaged the child and poisoned her with calomel and you have starved her. I shall have nothing more to do with it; take the child away and do as you like and if she dies you will have it on your conscience.'

Victoria turned to Stockmar for help. She asked him to tell Lehzen there had been a 'little misunderstanding' and the Queen was too upset to see anyone. He must also try and pacify Albert.

Albert knew who to blame. He told Stockmar: 'Lehzen is a crazy, common, stupid intriguer, obsessed with lust of power, who regards herself as a demi-god, and anyone who refuses to acknowledge her as such is a criminal.'

Victoria, he understood, had been brought up to regard Lehzen as an oracle. They had been bound together by their experiences in Kensington Palace. 'I on the other hand regard Victoria as naturally a fine character but warped in many respects by wrong upbringing.'

He had put up with a lot out of love and pity for Victoria, but he was not going to stand by and see his children and his marriage wrecked by the same person who had done so much damage to his wife as a child and young queen: 'There can be no improvement till Victoria sees Lehzen as she is, and I pray that this comes. But it seems like a curse upon our heads that Sir John… and indeed the whole world see the truth; and only the chief person concerned does not realize it, but regards the object of her infatuation as an angel and the world as suspicious, slanderous, envious…'

Victoria told Stockmar that she forgave Albert's 'thoughtless words' and begged him to speak up earlier when he found something amiss. This brought another tirade from Albert: 'All the disagreeableness I suffer comes from one and the same person and that is precisely the person whom Victoria chooses for her friend and confidante… Victoria is too hasty and passionate for me to be able often to speak of my difficulties. She will not hear me out but flies into a rage and overwhelms me with reproaches and suspiciousness, want of trust, ambition, envy etc. etc. There are, therefore, two ways open to me: (1) to keep silence and go away (in which case I am like a schoolboy who has had a dressing-down from his mother and goes off snubbed), (2) I can be still more violent (and then we have scenes… which I hate because I am so sorry for Victoria in her misery…).'

Stockmar grasped the nettle. He told Victoria that, if scenes like these recurred, he would have to leave Court. In other words, Victoria would have to choose between Lehzen and him.

Victoria responded that all she wanted to do was give Lehzen a quiet home for her past services that even Albert acknowledged. 'I assure you on my honour that I see her very seldom now and only for a few minutes, often to ask questions about papers and toilette for which she is of the greatest use to me. A. often thinks I see her when I don't… Our position is very different from any other married couple. A. is in my house and not I in his… Dearest Angel Albert, God knows how I love him. His position is difficult, heaven knows, and we must do everything to make it easier.'

Temper tantrums

She blamed herself. Since she was a child she had outbursts of anger which she called her 'combustibles'. These had to be tamed.

On 20 January 1842, she wrote: 'There is often an irritability in me which (like Sunday last which began the whole misery) makes me say cross & odious things which I don't believe myself & which I fear hurt A. but which he should not believe, but I will strive to conquer it though I knew before I married that this would be a trouble; I therefore wished not to marry, as the two years and a half, when I was so completely my own mistress made it difficult for me to control myself & to bend to another's will, but I trust I shall be able to conquer it.'

First the nursery would be reorganized. Melbourne suggested that it should be entrusted to a lady of rank and title. The position of superintendent of the royal nursery was offered to Lady Lyttelton, one of the ladies of the bedchamber who had five children of her own. She had little money and was grateful for employment in the palace. An admirer of the Prince, she agreed that Vicky had been fussed over too much and that the doctors were of little help.

On 25 July, Albert sacked Lehzen, merely telling his wife that she was going back to Germany in two months' time. Stockmar reassured Victoria that Lehzen needed rest and quiet for the sake of her health.

'I went to see my dear good Lehzen & found her very cheerful, saying she felt it was necessary for her health to go away, for of course, I did not require her so much now, & would find others to help me, whilst she could still help me in doing little things for me abroad,' wrote Victoria. 'She repeated, she would be ready to come to me, whenever I wanted, so that I can see her from time to time. Altogether, nothing could have been more satisfactory & pleasant than was our little interview. Walked out in the afternoon with Albert, & when we came home, we played on the piano.'

After dinner, Victoria 'felt rather bewildered & low, at what had

Rare early photograph of Victoria with Albert, 1851.

taken place, & naturally the thought of the coming separation from my dear Lehzen, whom I love so much, made me feel very sad.'

Lehzen departed without saying goodbye in person.

After breakfast on 30 September, Victoria wrote: 'I had a letter from my dear Lehzen in which she took leave of me in writing, thinking it would be less painful than seeing me & as the wind had abated, & everything was ready for her departure, she had started off at once. This naturally upset me, & I so regret not being able to embrace her once more, thought, on the other hand I am much relieved at being spared the painful parting. But I felt it very much. Though I had, in fact, seen but little of my dear good Lehzen since our marriage, still the thought that she was far away now, & all alone, made we very sad. I can never forget that she was for many years everything to me & I shall be forever grateful & devotedly attached to her. Still for herself & for all, she has done the wisest thing.'

Baroness Lehzen went to live with her sister in Bückeburg, near Hanover, with a generous pension of £800 a year – worth £80,000 ($104,000) today. Victoria gave her a carriage as a leaving present. Much has been made of an apparent estrangement between the Queen and her governess and later adviser and companion, but they continued to correspond regularly after her departure. In 1858, the Baroness waited on Bückeburg station to catch a glimpse as the train carrying Victoria and Albert to see their newly married daughter Vicky passed through. Then in 1866, after Albert had died, Victoria visited her in Reinhardsbrunn, where she was bedridden after fracturing a hip. She died in 1870, aged 85.

Ruling the roost

Albert now reigned supreme. He controlled Victoria's finances, had keys to her boxes and access to her ministers. As her de facto

Private Secretary, he read state papers, drafted letters, advised the Queen, frequently dominated meetings and was a major influence on the government through his accord with prime minister Sir Robert Peel. Meanwhile, he took up roles in institutions including the Royal Agricultural Society, the Philharmonic Society, the British Association, the Society for Improving the Condition of the Labouring Classes, the Statistical Congress of All Nations Conference, the National Education Conference, the Dublin Exhibition, the Great Exhibition, the Society of the Arts, the Society for the Extinction of Slavery and the Royal Commission for Fine Arts, and set about transforming his adopted country.

But despite all Albert's good works, he was not well liked, especially among Victoria's family who regarded him as something of an upstart. Victoria thought he deserved some recognition.

In June 1842, she spoke to Peel about 'dear Albert's awkward & painful position'. She pointed out that provisions were made for a Queen Consort and that the same should be true of a Prince Consort: 'It seemed to me very wrong that the reigning Queen's Husband should not have the same,' she said. 'Sir Robert Peel thought the reason was a fear that a Prince Consort might usurp the Queen's right. This I cannot agree in, but Sir Robert expressed his readiness & anxiety to do what he could, while deprecating a long discussion in Parliament, which might not make Albert's position more agreeable. I remarked that the position of a Prince Consort must be painful & humiliating to any man & that at times I almost felt it would have been fairer to him, for me not to have married him. But he was so good & kind & had loved me for myself.'

One of Victoria's great skills was to be able to change her mind and revise her opinions of people and of events. She had a 'vein of iron' as Lady Lyon once noted, but the iron could bend. The affinity between Albert and Sir Robert Peel had prompted her to re-evaluate her opinions of the current prime minister. Once she had referred to him as the 'cold odd man', but her opinion had much changed after their recent dealings and she said of him that he had become 'a great statesman, a man who thinks but little of party and never of himself.'

In February 1845, after five years of marriage, Victoria sought the title of King Consort for Albert, again unsuccessfully. Nevertheless, that December, when Lord Lansdowne and Lord John Russell visited Windsor, they were received by Victoria and Albert together. Charles Greville, clerk of the Privy Council noted: 'Both of them always said We… It is obvious that while she has the title he is really discharging the functions of the Sovereign. He is King to all intents and purposes.'

Finally, on 25 June 1857, Victoria used her royal prerogative to make Albert officially Prince Consort by letters patent. However, along the way Albert did pick up a few titles on the death of Victoria's Uncle Augustus, Duke of Sussex, in 1843, becoming Knight Great Master of the Order of the Bath and Governor of the Round Tower at Windsor Castle.

Chapter Nine

THE MODEL FAMILY

While Albert was an accomplished horseman, he did not take to trains. The dizzying speed of 44 miles an hour gave him motion sickness. The Queen took it in her stride. Of their first trip returning from Windsor to 'smoky London' on 17 February 1843, she said: 'I find the motion so very easy far more so, than a carriage, & cannot understand how anyone can suffer from it.'

Victoria gave birth to their second daughter on 25 April 1843. She was christened Alice Maud Mary, though she was known as 'Fatima' because she was fat: 'At 5 minutes past 4, a fine, healthy girl was born & all my sufferings had come to an end! The only person who was there, to whom the child could be shown, was Lord Liverpool,' Victoria said.

Albert had stopped the practice of having a dozen men of state waiting in the next room when the Queen gave birth. 'I felt extremely quiet and comfortable afterwards & slept a good deal. My beloved Albert, who had watched so tenderly over me the whole time had many people to see, & such numbers of letters to write.'

Albert sat with her that evening. She soon found it 'rather dull lying quite still & doing nothing, particularly in moments when one is alone'. But Albert was on hand again to push her bed into another room so she could have company. Soon they were going for long walks again, playing skittles, drinking cowslip wine and, in the evenings, reading by lamplight, while their children played on the floor. She enjoyed domestic life in Buckingham Palace and was particularly fond of the garden. When they left for Windsor on 3 August, she wrote: 'I have been so happy there (but where am I not happy now?).'

In January 1844, Albert's father died. Victoria shared his distress, writing in her journal: 'We feel so wretched & desolate, though comforted & happy, in the intense love we bear one another.'

He wrote to his brother Ernest: 'Our little children do not know why we cry and they ask us why we are in black; Victoria weeps with me, for me and for all of you. Let us take care of [our wives], let us love and protect them, as in them we shall find happiness again.'

Small consolations

Albert called Victoria a 'consoling angel': 'She is the treasure on which my whole existence rests,' he told Stockmar. 'The relation in which we stand to one another leaves nothing to desire. It is a union of heart and soul, and is therefore noble, and in it the poor children shall find their cradle, so as to be able one day to ensure a like happiness for themselves.'

The mood may have been lightened by the visit of General Tom Thumb to the palace. Just 25 inches tall, the American boy, named after a character from Arthurian legend but whose real name was Charles Sherwood Stratton, had stopped growing at seven months. Now six years old, he was something of a celebrity, employed by the circus impresario B.T. Barnum. Having toured the United States, he had been brought to Europe and was performing at several venues in London, in particular the Egyptian Hall in Piccadilly.

Dressing up in military uniform, he did impersonations, he sang and danced. Reviews were favourable, with *The Times* claiming that he was 'the most minute specimen of walking and talking humanity it is possible to conceive'.

The miniature man was invited to perform at the palace; at last, someone Victoria could look down on. 'He made the funniest little bow,' she said, 'putting out his hand & saying: "Much obliged, Mam".' This clear breach of etiquette raised a laugh.

She took him by the hand and walked him around the long picture gallery, which contained priceless paintings collected by Charles I, asking him questions. He put on a show for the royal household, imitating Napoleon and doing other tricks. But when it came to withdrawing backwards, he could not keep up with the others, would turn and run, then turning to back out again to more laughter.

'One cannot help feeling very sorry for the poor little thing & wishing he could be properly cared for, for the people who show him off tease him a good deal, I should think,' she said. It was the first of three trips to the palace. Victoria gave him money and gifts, and her royal patronage brought him prestige and publicity.

Separation

For the first time since they had married, Victoria and Albert were to be apart while he returned to Germany for two weeks. On 11 April 1844, Victoria recorded 'the immense joy of beholding my beloved Husband's dear face again, & being clasped in his arms. He is looking so well, & seemed & told me how happy he was to get back to me, for which I felt so grateful... The Children had welcomed their Father at the bottom of the stairs, & are so pleased to see him again. I had so much to tell him, & so much to ask about.'

The next day, she said: 'I did not sleep very well having been really too agitated with joy & thankfulness, at the safe return of my beloved Albert.'

On 6 August 1844, she gave birth to their second son, Alfred Ernest Albert, or Affie.

'The Baby has a quantity of long dark hair, which none of the others had, large blue eyes, & a large nose,' she wrote.

While Albert was busy overseeing the rebuilding of the Houses of Parliament, which had burnt down in 1834, and revising the curriculum as chancellor of Cambridge University, he did not neglect his domestic duties. His renovation of Buckingham Palace continued. He added a farm, a dairy and kennels to Windsor Castle, and designed Osborne House on the Isle of Wight as a summer retreat. Victoria had stayed on the island as a child and Albert bought the estate from his own allowance when Peel told him it was up for sale. The building work there was something he could do on his own without the interference of government departments. It was to be a labour of love.

Quickly realizing that the house as it was would be too small for their growing family, they decided to rebuild on the original footprint but with considerable extension. Albert brought in master builder Thomas Cubitt to help on the project, though he designed much of it himself. Construction of the whole estate, at its centre a large house in the style of an Italian Renaissance *palazzo*, began in 1845 and was finished by 1851. The resulting building, comprising four connecting blocks arranged around two courtyards and wide, grand terraces connected by flights of steps, was set off by two imposing Belvedere towers. It had a distinctly Mediterranean feel. From the flat Italianate roof, Victoria and Albert directed the landscaping of the ornate, formal gardens, a model farm, estate cottages, a sea wall to protect the seaward frontage of the estate and also a coastguard house. The surrounding parkland included

Windsor Castle – when Prince Albert died on 14 December 1861, the Blue Room where he died was kept just as it was the day he died, a state of affairs which lasted for 40 years.

21 miles of paths and walks. For the interior of the house, Albert also designed the cribs in the nursery, the lights over the billiard tables and sliding doors in the drawing room that were mirrored to reflect the light from the chandeliers. It was furnished with writing desks, portraits of the family and casts of the children's hands and feet. There, at Christmas, the family would sing hymns he had composed to the accompaniment of wind instruments and, at Easter, there would be Easter egg hunts.

In the yellow drawing room was the painting *La Siesta* by Franz Xaver Winterhalter, one of Victoria's favourite artists, and it is thought to be the first picture she bought. It shows three young women with dreamy expressions on their faces sitting in a sunlit bower. The painting was completed in 1841. Two years later, Winterhalter painted Victoria herself in full regalia and, in 1846, the four-year-old Bertie in a sailor suit.

Outside there was a Swiss Cottage, where the children played soldiers with a model fort and guns, and grew plants and kept their collection of rocks. Albert also built an icehouse and a small lake in case there was a fire.

On the small sandy beach overlooking the Solent, Albert built Victoria a semi-circular beach-hut with a mosaic floor and a domed ceiling of blue, pink and gold. On hot days, Victoria's bathing machine would be rolled out. Inside she would don voluminous bathing apparel by the light of two small frosted windows. She would then step out on to a curtained veranda and descend five wooden steps. Only when she was fully concealed by the water would the curtains be opened.

Perfect little paradise

Recalling her first plunge, Victoria wrote: 'Drove down to the beach with my maids & went into the bathing machines, where I undressed & bathed in the sea, (for the 1st time in my life) a very nice bathing woman attending me. I thought it delightful till I put my head under water, when I thought I should be stifled. After dressing again, drove back.'

But it was the surrounding countryside that Victoria loved. She called Osborne a 'perfect little Paradise'. In May 1845, she wrote: 'The walks here are endless, & the views of land & sea, lovely. It does one's heart good to see how my beloved Albert enjoys it all, & is so full of admiration of the place, & of all the places & improvements he means to carry out. He is hardly to be kept at home for a moment.'

Osborne House on the Isle of Wight as it is today.

It was a paradise for the children too. They dug potatoes in the garden, picked flowers in the woods where nightingales sang and watched the sheep being washed at a nearby farm.

The royal family were at Osborne when the Corn Laws, putting tariffs on foreign grain and hiking the price of bread, were repealed in March 1846 in the wake of the Irish Potato Famine. Victoria was just coming up from the beach when a servant arrived with the news in a box from the House of Commons. However, Peel had expended all his political capital in the effort. On the same night the bill was passed in the House of Lords, 25 June, Peel's Irish Coercion Bill, which aimed to suppress discontent in Ireland, was defeated in the Commons by a combination of Whigs, Radicals and Tory protectionists. Peel resigned. He visited them at Osborne House to tell them the news. Victoria had grown rather fond of him, recording in her diary: 'His loss is an immense one, to us, to the Country, & to all Europe & I tremble for the future, & for the consequences it may bring.'

Meanwhile, Victoria had given birth to a fifth child, Helena Augusta Victoria, at Buckingham Palace on 25 May. The German nickname for Helena was 'Helenchen', later shortened to Lenchen, the name by which members of the royal family invariably referred to her. Her birth made Victoria more sanguine about the political upheavals: 'Really when one is so happy & blessed in one's home life, as I am, Politics (provided my Country is safe) must take only a 2nd place,' she wrote.

The Lady of the Lions

Albert was known for his highbrow tastes and they sang along when Felix Mendelssohn gave private concerts. They also built a private theatre so they could watch plays at home. But the Queen also had a penchant for more lowbrow entertainment. 'The Lady of the Lions', Nellie Chapman – who entered cages of lions and tigers, putting her head in their mouths, and emerged unscathed – performed in the courtyard of Windsor Castle. The Queen met her and the circus proprietor 'Lord' George Sanger afterwards. Billed as 'the tallest couple in the world', the pair were invited to Buckingham Palace after the announcement of their engagement. Victoria presented the couple with a wedding dress and a diamond ring. She also enjoyed going out to the circus, particularly to see the clowns and trick horseback riding.

But it wasn't all fun and games. On 30 December 1847, Victoria recorded that Albert had left Windsor at four o'clock after having lunch with the children, the first time since Christmas, to see a play in London, returning at 12.30 a.m. 'The evening appeared to me terribly long, all alone,' she said.

Still, Victoria was not unhappy. The following night she recorded: 'This is the last day of this year & I have thought much on all that has passed. When one is as happy as we are, one feels sad at the quick passing of the years, & I always wish Time could stand still for a while. This year has brought us much to be thankful for; the Children are so well, & the 2 eldest decidedly so improved. I have thought over my faults, – what I have to avoid, & what to correct, & with God's help & perseverance on my part I hope to conquer my shortcomings.'

Despite her previous outbursts, Victoria was thankful for Albert's help in the nursery. When a nurse had trouble in getting a glove on the hand of the two-and-a-half-year-old Bertie, Lady Lyttelton wrote: 'It was pretty to see him just coax the child on to his own knee, and put it on, without a moment's delay, by his great dexterity and gentle manner; the Princey, quite evidently glad to be so helped, looking up very softly at his father's beautiful face. It was a picture of a nursery scene. I could not help saying: "It is not every Papa who would have the patience and kindness," and got such a flashing look of gratitude from the Queen!'

Otherwise Albert sought to 'superintend the principles' of the children's upbringing, which was difficult 'in the face of so many women'. As they grew older, he took them to Madame Tussauds, the zoo and the theatre. He would play them silly songs on the organ, fly kites with them or turn somersaults.

'He is so kind to them,' wrote Victoria, 'and romps with them so delightfully, and manages them so beautifully and firmly.'

Death threats

He also taught them himself for an hour a day and dedicated himself to their security during a time when there were eight assassination attempts on Queen Victoria and death threats to the children came through the post. The Queen herself visited her children daily and spent hours with her babies. They romped in her dressing room while she was changing: 'Children, though often a source of anxiety & difficulty, are a great blessing & cheer & brighten up life,' she wrote.

Having left the louche behaviour of the Georgians behind, Victoria and Albert sought to cultivate the image of the model family. They established the elements of the middle-class monarchy that exists today. They had first travelled to Scotland in 1842, while she was struggling with post-natal depression after the birth of Bertie. Victoria enjoyed walking in the untamed grandeur of the landscape there. It reminded Albert of his childhood home in Germany.

They returned in 1844 to stay at Blair Castle and again in 1847, when they rented Ardverikie by Loch Laggan. During that trip, the weather was extremely rainy, which led Sir James Clark, the

Queen's physician, to recommend Deeside instead, for its dryer and more pleasant climate.

When Sir Robert Gordon died in 1847, his lease on Balmoral reverted to Lord Aberdeen. In February 1848, an arrangement was made – Prince Albert would acquire the remaining part of the castle's lease, together with its furniture and staff, without having seen the property first. The royal couple first visited in September 1848 and saw 'a pretty little Castle, in the old Scotch style... In front are a nice lawn & garden, with a high wooded hill behind, & at the back, there is a wood. The hills rise all around. One enters a nice little hall, & comes to a billiard room & Dining Room. A good broad staircase takes one upstairs & above the Dining room is our sitting room (formerly the Drawing room), a fine large room opening into our bedroom, &c.'

Victoria fell in love with the place immediately: 'We lunched directly & then walked up to the top of the wooded hill, opposite our windows, where there is a cairn, from which there is a pretty winding path. The view was beautiful, – below was the house, to the left or rather behind, were the fine range of hills near Lochnagar, & to the right, towards Ballater, the valley of the Dee, with the river winding along. It was so calm & so solitary as one gazed around, that it did one good & seemed to breathe freedom & peace making one forget the world & its sad turmoil. There were some slight showers, but nothing to signify. When we came down we walked along the Dee, which is behind the house. I come in, Albert was going to try his luck with some stags, which were lying quite close to the house, as they come down of an evening, – but he was not successful.'

Two days later, they walked up the cairn, covering five miles. 'I felt as if I could have walked another 5. We got up higher even than

Craig Gowan, & the views were glorious. It was wonderful not seeing a human being, nor hearing a sound, excepting that of the wind, or the call of blackcock or grouse. It filled me with peculiar feelings of admiration & solemnity.'

At home in the Highlands

Being shy and introverted, Albert enjoyed not seeing a human face, but Victoria spent time chatting with the locals in the mud cottages: 'All the Highlanders are so free from anything like bluster, so straightforward, – no flattery, so simple, & honest,' she wrote. They are never vulgar, never take liberties, are so intelligent, modest & well bred.'

During regular visits over the next months, the royal couple threw themselves into Highland life. They wore tartan and Albert studied Gaelic, while the Queen and the children learned Scottish country dancing. Greville said: 'They live there without any state whatever; they live not merely like private gentlefolks, but like very small gentlefolks; small house, small rooms, small establishments.'

In 1852, when the purchase of the estate at Balmoral was complete, it was obvious that the existing castle was too small for Victoria and Albert's growing family and the social needs of a royal household. So, they took the decision to build a brand-new castle. Albert engaged the services of William Smith, the city architect of Aberdeen and the son of John Smith who had designed the earlier castle. Plans were drawn up to build some 100 yards from the existing buildings so that the family could live in them while construction took place. Work began in 1853. The new castle had two main blocks housing offices and the royal and guest apartments, each with central courtyards, that were linked by two-storey wings to a 100-foot-high clock tower. The baronial style building was finished off with round towers, turrets and a grand carriage porch.

For the rest of her life, Balmoral would remain the place where Victoria was happiest and she would tell everyone who would listen of her love of Highland life. There she could mix with ordinary people, enjoy nature in all its glory and take long walks in the wild terrain. It was a world away from the stuffy formality that prevailed, even at her beloved Osborne.

Chapter Ten

UNDER THREAT

In 1848, Victoria's fears for the future were realized as revolutions spread across Europe. That year witnessed a wave of political upheaval across much of the Continent, with over 50 countries affected. The unrest was sparked by a perfect storm of political causes, which resulted in tens of thousands of deaths. In essence, the uprisings were attempting to end the old feudal structures, to curtail the power of royalty and to set up parliamentary democracies in their place. The discontent was widespread. A series of crop failures across the Continent during 1845–46 had caused increased hardship for rural peasants and the working urban poor. Sharply rising prices added to poor living conditions and, in many places, outbreaks of hunger-related disease prompted a radicalization of political attitudes.

The revolutions began in Sicily in January. But it was in France that matters escalated when the 'February Revolution' ended the monarchy of Louis-Philippe and led to the setting up of the Second Republic. News of the events was quickly carried around Europe via the newly invented telegraph and by the fast-expanding popular press. Trouble spread as others took up the causes in Germany, Austria, Italy, Hungary and further afield. Long-held prejudices and simmering discontent prompted widespread violence and social chaos. There was an upsurge in nationalism and consequently in prejudice against foreigners and, in particular, those of noble standing.

On 3 April, Victoria wrote in her journal: 'uncertainty everywhere, as well as for the future of our children, unarmed me, & I quite gave way to my grief... I feel grown 20 years older, & as if I could not anymore think of any amusement. I tremble at the thought of what may possibly await us here.'

King Louis-Philippe of France and his Sicilian-born wife Maria Amalia had been forced to flee for their lives. They were smuggled out of the country by the British consul and arrived at Buckingham Palace on 7 March with nothing but the clothes they stood up in. They took up residence at Claremont, while their daughter Clémentine and her husband, August of Saxe-Coburg and Gotha, a cousin of Albert's, stayed on in Buckingham Palace along with their children. Clémentine was the same age as Victoria and pregnant for the fourth time. She had suffered terribly during the flight. Her sister-in-law, Hélène, had her children – one of which was the heir to the throne – torn from her grasp by a mob.

'What could be more dreadful,' wrote Victoria. 'Poor Clém says she can't get to sleep, constantly seeing before her those horrible faces, & hearing these dreadful cries & shrieks. Then she said how melancholy were the thoughts of the future which God knows they are, if one tries to imagine the situation of the poor Royal Family... One can hardly grasp the desolation & misery of their most undeserved position.'

A crushed rose
Victoria and Clémentine would become close. Another daughter-in-law of Louis-Philippe, Princess Victoire of Saxe-Coburg-Gotha, a cousin of Victoria's, had such a reverse of fortune she was 'like a crushed rose', Victoria said. In the midst of making provision for

her extended family, Victoria had given birth to a fourth daughter, Louise Caroline Alberta, on 18 March. On her first birthday, Victoria wrote: 'May God bless the dear little child, who is so fat, strong, & well again. She was born in the most eventful times, & ought to be something peculiar in consequence.'

There were fears that the revolutions of 1848 would not be confined to the Continent. There was unrest in Ireland and when the Chartists, calling for political reform, announced a mass meeting on Kennington Common in south London on 10 April, the royal family fled London for Osborne in fear of their lives. Victoria wrote: 'The sorrow at the state of Germany, – at the distress & ruin all round, added to very bad news from Ireland, & alarm in people's minds at the great meeting which is to take place in London on the 10th, are trying my poor Albert very much.'

The idea was that working men from all over the country would assemble in one place, carried there by the new 1840s railway system, and march to parliament and deliver a powerful petition calling for universal male suffrage and other democratic reforms. The organizers hoped for 200,000 people. The authorities, under the Duke of Wellington, took no chances and cavalry and infantry, some 10,000 strong, were stationed around the common and on the bridges that separated it from parliament. Cannons were readied to protect Buckingham Palace and over 100,000 citizens were sworn in as special constables to assist the massed ranks of police on duty.

As it was, the Chartists' meeting went off peacefully, with only 25,000 or so in attendance. The speakers were unable to rouse the crowd and in pouring rain and an atmosphere of despondency and failure they wandered peacefully away from the scene. The authorities did allow a petition containing signatures to be delivered to the Houses of Parliament, but the Chartist movement was effectively over at that moment. However, the fear lingered. After they returned to London, Victoria and Albert were coming home from the opera when 'a man ran up to the carriage on Albert's side, where the window was open, saying several times over something like "a real murderer". This frightened me dreadfully, on account of the Chartist troubles & I could not get over it for some time.'

At 8.20 a.m. on 1 May 1850, their third son, Arthur, was born at Buckingham Palace. He was named after Arthur Wellesley, Duke of Wellington, whose birthday he shared. He became Victoria's favourite. She said he was 'dearer than the rest put together'.

While Victoria and Albert tried to keep an eye on how the political situation was developing abroad, they were hampered to such an extent by the foreign secretary Lord Palmerston that she refused to see him socially and was delighted when he was dismissed in 1851, though he returned to the Cabinet as home secretary the following year. Meanwhile, the royal couple were at odds politically. Victoria wanted to quash dissent, while Albert sought to address the problems that caused it.

Hard times

The British royal family survived the Year of Revolutions, but were soon shrouded in grief again. In November 1849, George Anson died at just 37. Albert mourned him like a brother. The following month Queen Adelaide, Victoria's aunt, passed on. On 2 July 1850, Robert Peel died after being thrown from a horse. Victoria said it was as if Albert had lost a second father. A week later, Victoria's uncle, the Duke of Cambridge, died. In August, Louis-Philippe died at Claremont. And in October, Uncle Leopold's beloved second wife, Louise of Orléans, died.

Throughout it all, Victoria was plagued with insomnia, put on weight and suffered a grievous assault. After visiting Cambridge

House in Piccadilly to see her dying uncle, the carriage in which she and three of her children were travelling back to the palace was surrounded by a crowd of well-wishers. A man, who Victoria had previously seen in the park, stepped forward and struck her in the face with a partridge cane: 'I felt myself violently thrown by a blow to the left of the carriage,' she said. 'My impulse had been to throw myself that way, not knowing what was coming next… My bonnet was crushed, & on putting my hand up to my forehead, I felt an immense bruise in the right side, fortunately well above the temple & eye! The man was instantly caught by the collar, & when I got up in the carriage, having quite recovered myself, & telling the good people who anxiously surrounded me, "I am not hurt", I saw him being violently pulled about by the people. Poor Fanny was so overcome, that she began to cry.'

There was consternation when she got home: 'Went upstairs to my room, to put arnica on my poor head, which was becoming very painful. The Children were much shocked, & poor Bertie turned very red at the time. It is the 2nd time that Alice & Affie have witnessed such an event. Thank God! they are never touched, — that indeed I could not bear with composure. Dearest Albert returned in 20 m. & was dreadfully shocked, annoyed & joined. All my people so distressed, some, quite crying.'

The Queen bore a small scar on her forehead for the next decade. The attack certainly unsettled her: 'Certainly, it is very hard & very horrid, that I, a woman – a defenceless young woman & surrounded by my Children, should be exposed to insults of this kind, & be unable to go out quietly for a drive,' she wrote. 'This is by far the most disgraceful & cowardly thing that has ever been done; for a man to strike any woman is most brutal & I, as well as everyone else, think this for worse than an attempt to shoot, which, wicked as it is, is at least more comprehensible & more courageous.'

Despite this, within two hours she attended the opera at Covent Garden to show that she bravely refused to let injury prevent her from going out among her subjects.

The culprit was former army officer Robert Pate. He was a gentleman and well known around Piccadilly for his peculiar gait and dandy style of dress. However, at his trial the court heard that Pate had shown signs of 'lunacy', having resigned his commission in 1846, and had subsequently become a recluse. He was sentenced to seven years in the penal colony in Van Diemen's Land, renamed Tasmania in 1856.

Stepping back

Despite her show of bravery at the opera, Victoria was now keen to withdraw from public life. With her permission, Albert now reigned on his own as acting monarch. And 1851 would see one of his greatest achievements – the construction of the Crystal Palace in Hyde Park for the opening of the Great Exhibition. Victoria wrote: 'Albert's dearest name is immortalized with this great conception. It was the happiest, proudest day of my life and I can think of nothing else.'

Although originally the idea of Henry Cole, a record keeper at the Public Records Office and a member of the Society of Arts, it was Prince Albert whose support led to the staging of the Great Exhibition, which has come to be regarded as one of the defining events of the 19th century. Built of glass and iron, the Crystal Palace, as it became known, was to house exhibits from all over the world to show off every marvel of the Victorian age: including pottery, porcelain, ironwork, furniture, perfumes, pianos, firearms, fabrics, steam hammers, hydraulic presses and even cutting-edge houses. It was a triumph; between May and October that year over six million visitors passed through the crystal doors. Profits from

Queen Victoria opening the Great Exhibition at the Crystal Palace in London, 1851.

the exhibition were used to build a complex of museums in South Kensington as well as Imperial College for Science, the Royal Colleges of Art and Music and the Albert Hall.

The Queen did not seem to mind being side-lined by Albert's triumph. On 3 February 1852, she wrote to her Uncle Leopold, saying: 'Albert grows daily fonder and fonder of politics and business, and is so wonderfully fit for both – such perspicacity and such courage – and I grow daily to dislike them more and more... We women are not made for governing – and if we are good women, we must dislike these masculine occupations; but there are times which force one to take an interest in them *mal gre ban gre* [sic: "whether one likes it or not"], and I do, of course, intensely.'

She was now content to be a wife and mother. Another son, Leopold, was born on 7 April 1853. During labour, she took chloroform for the first time. For once, she did not suffer the agonies of childbirth: 'The effect was soothing, quieting & delightful beyond measure,' she said.

It was later discovered that Leopold suffered from haemophilia. Victoria carried the gene, which is transmitted by women but only affects males. This would have disastrous consequences for the history of Europe.

The thin and sickly baby put an extra strain on Victoria and she began to have hysterical outbursts, caused by 'imprudently heaping up a pile of combustibles', Albert said. He sought to tackle the situation by writing a long and patronizing memo to her, saying:

Dear Child,
Now it will be the right to consider calmly the facts of the
case. The whole offence which led to continuance of hysterics

for more than an hour, and the traces of which have remained for more than 24 hours more, was: that I complained of your turning several times from inattention the wrong leaves in a Book which was to be [used] by us as a Register... of prints... This miserable trifle produced the distressing scene... in which I am accused of making things worse by my false method of treatment. I admit that my treatment has on this occasion as on former ones signally failed, but I know of no other... When I try to demonstrate the groundlessness and injustice of the accusations which are brought against me I increase your distress... But I never intend or wish to offend you... If you are violent I have no other choice but to leave you... I leave the room and retire to my own room in order to give you time to recover yourself. Then you follow me to renew the dispute and to have it all out... Now don't believe that I do not sincerely and deeply pity you for the sufferings you undergo, or that I deny you do really suffer very much, I merely deny that I am the cause of them, though I have unfortunately often been the occasion... I am often astonished at the effect which a hasty word of mine has produced...

In your candid way, you generally explain later what was the real cause of your complaint... It appears now that the apprehension that you might be made answerable for the suffering of the Baby (occasioned by the milk of the Wet nurse not agreeing on account of your having frequently expressed a wish to have a Nurse from the Highlands of Scotland) was the real cause of your distress which broke out on the occasion of the Registration of the prints.

While Victoria recorded in her diary Albert's 'untiring love, tenderness and care', he complained that he was being accused of 'want of feeling, hard heartedness, injustice, hatred, jealousy, distrust, etc., etc.' With his busy life, there were difficulties of communication. In another letter, which he wrote to her in February 1855, he asked: 'What can I do to you, save, at the most, not listen to you long enough when I have business elsewhere?'

Happy times

Despite these travails Victoria counted her blessings. On her 34th birthday, she wrote: 'Was awoke by the Band playing the Hymn "Now Thank We All Our God", a little before 7, & was so tenderly & lovingly congratulated by my precious Husband, who I fervently pray & confidently trust God will preserve for many a year to me! What blessings do I not enjoy! often I feel surprised at being so loved, & tremble at my great happiness, dreading that I may be too happy! May I show daily more & more my gratitude to our Heavenly Father, & may He ever protect us, our dear Children & my dear Country. May He also preserve my dear Mother & all our dear ones, for years to come!'

Since the Duchess of Kent had moved out of the royal household, the breach with Victoria has gradually been closed and mother and daughter were now reconciled. When Conroy died in 1854, the Duchess wrote to Victoria, saying: '[He] has been of great use to me, but unfortunately has also done great harm.' And she asked her daughter to put the past behind them along with the 'passions of those who stood between us'.

There were grave matters of state to attend to. At the outbreak of the Crimean War in October 1853, Victoria wrote: 'On such an occasion one feels wretched at being a woman though my heart is not in this unsatisfactory war.'

But when the Scots Fusiliers marched past the palace on their way to Portsmouth, she said: 'I shall never forget the touching, beautiful sight.' The sappers and miners came through the gates into the courtyard, where they presented arms and gave three hearty cheers, 'which went straight to my heart'. Then, as the casualties mounted, Victoria told her Uncle Leopold: 'My whole soul and heart are in the Crimea.'

She did her best to keep abreast of news from the battlefields. A year after the war began, she interviewed a Lieutenant Colonel Jeffreys who had recently returned. He told her of 'the misery, the suffering, the total lack of everything, the sickness, &c.'

Victoria feared that the newspaper reports of the British shortcomings served to encourage the Russians. After her interview with Jeffreys, she wrote in her journal: 'He admitted that this was a great misfortune, but that on the other hand they felt certain things ought to be made known, else they would not be remedied, & the country must understand what has been going on… The trenches, badly drained, were full of water so that one had to lie up to one's waist in it. This was even the case with the Officers, who hardly had had time to change their boots, being constantly obliged to turn out in the night. What must it then have been with the poor men? They had to lie down in their wet clothes, frequently being unable to change them for 1 or 2 nights. They froze & when they did pull off their boots, portions of their feet would come off with them! This Col. Jeffreys himself had seen, & could therefore declare to be no exaggeration of the newspapers.'

Victoria plainly felt deeply for the men who fought, suffered and died in her name. She visited the hospitals to see soldiers with bullet wounds, missing limbs, disfigured by frostbite and toothless from scurvy: 'One could not wish the war to have continued when one looked on these brave, noble fellows, so cruelly mutilated & suffering!' she wrote.

She did what she could, writing to the Duke of Newcastle, the Secretary of State for War: 'The Queen feels it to be one of her highest prerogatives and dearest duties to care for the welfare and success of the army,' she wrote. However, she had her misgivings, saying, after reading despatches from Lord Raglan, commander in chief in Crimea: 'I am so little versed in military matters, that I shall be unable adequately to describe what the difficulties consist in, but will try to put down in a few words, what I mean.' She was happiest giving out medals, instituting the Victoria Cross for gallantry, and invited Florence Nightingale to stay at Balmoral.

Initially, the war, which involved an alliance between Britain, France and the Ottoman Empire fighting to deny Russia gaining territory and power at Ottoman expense, did not go well. Huge casualties were sustained by the allies during the Battle of Balaclava in October 1854. The winter proved disastrous, for the British army in particular, as storms sank 30 transport ships and another vessel carrying winter clothing. The troops suffered from sickness and the freezing temperatures. Colonel Jeffreys had been correct. For his failures as head of the war department, Newcastle suffered the wrath of the nation early in 1855 and resigned in disgrace on 1 February.

At the same time parliament passed a bill to investigate the conduct of the war, as a result of which the prime minister, Lord Aberdeen, resigned. Victoria had never liked the high-handed foreign secretary Lord Palmerston, who she felt took no notice of her, so she asked Lord Derby to form a government, but when Palmerston refused to serve as minister of war, Derby gave up. She then asked the Marquess of Lansdowne, but he was too old. She asked Lord John Russell, but none of his former colleagues except

Palmerston would serve under him. So, she had no alternative but to summon the 70-year-old Palmerston, as he was the only one of her ministers considered capable of leading the country to victory. Within a year, the war was over and Palmerston was appointed to the Order of the Garter.

Chapter Eleven

MY DUTY... AS A WOMAN

Albert celebrated the fall of Sevastopol to the allied forces in September 1855, which effectively ended war in the Crimea, by climbing to the top of Craig Gowan where a bonfire was lit. Victoria watched from Balmoral. The pipes were played. There was dancing and guns were fired. Albert said the scene was 'wild & exciting beyond everything. Healths had been drunk amidst great enthusiasm.'

However, the war had led to a renewed antipathy to foreigners and Albert's brief popularity began to wane again. This upset Victoria who urged her ministers to support her husband. They were only too happy to do so as, in the manner of the day, he and they considered him superior to her, by dint of being a man. Albert wrote to his brother: 'That you are frequently in society including excellent artists is pleasing to hear. However, I cannot agree that you can only gain in conversation with brilliant/clever ladies/women. You will lack in manliness and clarity of your perceptions of the world; for the more brilliant those ladies are, the more confused they are about general ideas and principles. I would prefer to see you in close and intimate traffic with older men who are experienced in life and have achieved something and reached a balance within themselves and with humanity in general.'

Albert happily lectured Victoria on the need for 'improvement' and she now called him her 'Lord & Master'. On 10 February 1854, she wrote: 'The 14th anniversary of this ever-blessed day was ushered in with music, & with the never failing tender love of my beloved Albert! Few women are so blessed with such a Husband, & May God continue to protect us for many, many years!'

He gave her a bracelet to mark the day and she dug out her marriage lines: 'Read over the marriage service, containing certainly some very fine passages. I feel so impressed by the promise I made "to love, cherish, honour, serve & obey" my Husband. May it ever be duly impressed on my mind, & on that of every woman.'

And she put herself down. On the 18th anniversary of her accession, she wrote: 'I trust I have tried to do my duty, though I feel how incompetent, I, as a woman, am, to what I ought to be. I often think what a blessing it would be, were dearest Albert King, instead of me!'

On Albert's 35th birthday, she called him 'the dearest, best, & purest of beings, who is a blessing not only to me, but also to this land, for without him what should I & the country have done! Yet I often feel how unworthy I am, though no wife ever loved & worshipped her husband as I do! May God bless & ever protect him & may we long be spared to one another!'

At seven o'clock the band struck up Albert's own hymn. 'Dressed in a new white & pink muslin, & saw to all being ready in the present room. Then hastened to fetch my beloved one. The 8 Children were in the corridor of the other part of the house. The present room was very prettily decorated much in the same style as mine was. Amongst my gifts were a picture of Leopold, by Winterhalter, as a pendant to the one of Arthur with a ball, a painting by C. Haag of McDonald going through the Dee with Affie on his shoulder & leading Bertie, on the day of the salmon spearing. The Children had each drawn, worked, & written out, everything they could think of to please their dear Father. Mama was there & breakfasted with us, during which time the Band played. Afterwards Affie played 2 or 3 things on the violin, Vicky a very pretty piece on the piano, Alice, the same, Bertie a short piece.'

Friedrich, the only son of Wilhelm I, King of Prussia and later the first emperor of Germany, was staying at Balmoral in 1855 when he asked if he could marry Vicky, then 14. Victoria was thrilled, but Vicky was not to be told until she turned 16 and had been confirmed. 'He is a dear, excellent, charming young man, whom we shall give our dear child to with perfect confidence. What pleases us greatly is to see he is really delighted with Vicky,' Victor told Uncle Leopold.

Baby number nine

In 1856, Victoria was pregnant, again – and complaining about it, again. Albert wrote to her, saying: 'I, like everyone else in the house make the most ample allowance for your state… We cannot, unhappily, bear your bodily sufferings for you – you must struggle with them alone – the moral ones are probably caused by them, but if you were rather less occupied with yourself and your feelings and took more interest in the outside world, you would find that the greatest help of all.'

Victoria's ninth child, Beatrice, was born on 14 April 1857, again with the use of chloroform. Having so many babies had taken its toll. She was nearly 38 and Dr Clark advised that this should be her last child. 'Can I have no more fun in bed?' she asked the physician.

The pregnancy had been gruelling. She had a bad cough and was grieving for her half-brother, Carl Leiningen, who died in November 1856. Albert told his brother that Victoria was 'hardly able to do what is expected of her'. Nevertheless, just two weeks after giving birth to Beatrice, she said: 'I have felt better & stronger this time, than I have ever done before. How I also thank God for granting us such a dear, pretty girl, which I so much wished for!'

This time she felt genuine affection from the beginning. Going up to see the tot in her bath, she said: 'A greater duck, you could not see & she is such a pet of her Papa's, stroking his face with her 2 dear little hands.'

On Beatrice's first birthday, Victoria wrote: 'No words can express what that sweet, pretty, intelligent little creature, is to us!'

Harsh disciplinarian

Nevertheless, she continued to be a strict mother, once beating her haemophiliac son Leopold so hard that her mother begged her to stop and asked how she could bear to hear her children cry so much. 'Once you've had nine, Mother, you don't notice any more,' she replied.

Albert was saddened by his wife's attitude. He disciplined his children too, but also loved playing with them: 'It is a pity you find no consolation in the company of your children,' he wrote to her. 'The root of the trouble lies in the mistaken notion that the function of a mother is always to be correcting, scolding and ordering them about and organizing their activities. It is not possible to be on happy friendly terms with people you have just been scolding.'

Meanwhile, the Indian Mutiny had broken out. This uprising was against the rule of the British East India Company, which functioned as a sovereign power on behalf of the British Crown. The rebellion was caused by invasive social reforms, harsh land taxes, and disapproval of other 'improvements' brought about by British rule, and was notable for exceptional cruelty by both sides. Hearing of the massacre of women and children at Cawnpore (now Kanpur), Victoria wrote: 'One's blood runs cold, & one's heart bleeds. Many have succeeded in escaping, but after unheard of sufferings & having lost all. And that this should happen after years of tranquillity & security!'

She found it difficult to sleep for thinking about it and she asked Lady Canning, a former lady-in-waiting then wife of the governor of India, to extend her sympathies to the families of the victims – 'A woman and above all a wife and mother can only too well enter into the agonies gone thro' of the massacres.' She was also appalled by the savage reprisals taken by British soldiers, telling Lord Canning: 'They should know there is no hatred to a brown skin – none.'

When the British finally re-established control, Victoria let it be known that she wanted the religious beliefs of her Indian subjects to be respected and that jobs be open to all, regardless of race, class or creed.

As the Indian Mutiny was coming to a close, Vicky married Friedrich, Prince of Prussia, in the Chapel Royal in St James's Palace on 25 January 1858. Although it was a joyful occasion, Victoria confided to her diary: 'The flourish of trumpets & cheering of thousands, made my heart sink within me, & I could hardly command myself.'

Eight days later, the newly-weds left for Berlin: 'We went into the Audience Room where Mama & all the Children were assembled & here poor Vicky's & Alice's, as well as other's tears began to flow fast,' Victoria recalled. 'Still I struggled but as I came to the staircase my breaking heart gave way… Also amongst the many servants there, I don't think there was a dry eye. Poor dear Child, she kissed 1st one, then the other, shaking hands with many. I clasped her in my arms, not knowing what to say & kissed good Fritz, pressing his hand again & again. He was quite unable to speak for emotion. Again, at the door of carriage I embraced them both.' Later at tea, she said 'my grief again burst forth'. Albert accompanied Vicky to the Royal Yacht at Gravesend, where Vicky broke down completely.

The minutiae of life

Victoria wanted to know every detail of her daughter's new life. She wrote telling her to 'give me your feelings – and your impressions about people and things, and little interior details. 1st: What dress and bonnet did you wear on landing? And what bonnet the next 2 days? 2nd: What sort of rooms had you at Cologne and Magdeburg? 3rd: Did you dine with your people at Cologne and did you sup at Magdeburg at 12? 4th: What cloak did you wear on the road, and have you been drawing? 5th: How do you like the German diet – and how do your poor maids bear this hurry scurry?'

Victoria could not give up her role as a martinet of a mother. She told her daughter not to stoop, to clean her teeth, not to laugh too loud or drink too much, eat more during the day, but beware of getting fat. 'So, you see dear, that though alas far away (which I shall never console myself for) – I watch over you as if I were there,' Victoria wrote.

Soon a letter came saying Vicky was pregnant. Victoria dashed off a reply, saying: 'The horrid news has upset us dreadfully.' Nevertheless, she upbraided her daughter for choosing a delivery date when she could not be with her. Instead, she sent Dr Clark and his chloroform, along with a midwife.

On 27 January 1859, Victoria became a grandmother when Vicky gave birth to the future Kaiser Wilhelm II. Now Victoria ordered the bells rung at Windsor and fireworks. Vicky sent her a locket containing a lock of her grandson's hair. Victoria took a great interest in every detail of Vicky's recovery. It was only when her daughter came to visit that May that she learnt that a breech birth had left the child with a withered left arm, which would lead him to resent his mother. Despite this, as time went on, Victoria became a doting grandmother.

The birth of the child forged a new bond between mother and daughter. On her visit, they walked in the gardens of Buckingham Palace, talking earnestly: 'We so completely understand one another,' wrote Victoria. 'She is a dear, clever, good affectionate child, & we are like 2 sisters!'

Their new-found friendship would not get in the way of the affairs of state though. Victoria took time off to read telegrams announcing the defeat of the Austrians by Franco-Italian forces in the Battle of Palestro before taking Vicky to sit for her favourite artist Franz Winterhalter.

She was still full of motherly advice. Vicky should not risk neglecting her husband for the sake of her children – 'No lady, and still less a Princess overdid the passion for the nursery.' She herself claimed that she only saw her youngest children bathed and put to bed four times a year. But it was to Vicky that she confided her unhappy childhood and her great love of Albert. 'He was my father, my protector, my guide and adviser in all and everything, my mother (I might almost say) as well as my husband,' she told her daughter in a letter. 'I suppose no one ever was so completely altered and changed in every way as I was by dearest Papa's blessed influence. Papa's position towards me is therefore of a very peculiar character and when he is away I feel quite paralyzed.'

The problem with Bertie

On the other hand, she felt 'wretched' about 16-year-old Bertie. He was lazy, ignorant, dull and ugly, 'with that painfully small and narrow head, those immense features and total want of chin'. He was putting on weight, had a large mouth and a hanging 'Coburg nose' like his mother's, and he had had his hair cut short and parted in the middle which 'makes him appear to have no head and all face'.

When Vicky told her mother that Bertie had been charming on his visit to Germany, she fired back: 'I think him very dull; his other three brothers are all so amusing and communicative.'

The diplomat, Lord Clarendon, who was charged with looking after Bertie on an early trip to Paris, said he thought 'the Queen's severe way of treating her children very injudicious'.

She had a more rounded view of her son Leopold, saying: 'He is tall, but holds himself worse than ever, and is a very common looking child, very plain in face, clever but an oddity – and not an engaging child, though amusing.' Elsewhere she called him 'a clever, honest & well-intentioned boy'. And speaking of Arthur, she said: 'Children are a great comfort to me at times, for their innocent unconsciousness is refreshing and cheering to one's heart.'

Helena also came in for criticism. Her features were 'so very large and long that it spoils her looks'. She felt she had the right to complain about her offspring as she had suffered so much to bring them into the world. When Vicky wrote that a married woman was more at liberty in society than an unmarried one, Victoria lamented: 'Aches – and sufferings and miseries and plagues – which you must struggle against – and enjoyments etc. to give up – constant precautions to take, you will feel the yoke of a married woman... I had 9 times for eight months to bear with those above-named enemies and I own it tired me sorely; one feels so pinned down – one's wings clipped – in fact, at the best... only half oneself – particularly the first and second time. This I call the "shadow side" as much as being torn away from one's loved home, parents and brothers and sisters. And therefore, I think our sex a most unenviable one.'

Even the angelic Albert sometimes sneered at her and other women's bodily woes. She could even be quite critical: 'That despising our poor, degraded sex is a little in all clever men's natures,' she wrote to Vicky, 'dear Papa even is not quite exempt though he would not admit it – but he laughs and sneers constantly at many of them and at our unavoidable inconveniences, etc., though he hates the want of affection, of due attention to and protection of them, says that the men who leave all home affairs – and the education of their children to their wives – forget their first duties.'

When Albert refused to let Victoria take her younger children with her to see Vicky in Prussia in 1858, she said he was a 'hard-hearted and great tyrant'. Soon after, the 14-year-old Prince Alfred was posted to the steam frigate HMS *Euryalus*. When he left on his first voyage to the Mediterranean, South Africa and the West Indies, returning home in 1861, she told Vicky: 'Papa is most cruel upon the subject. I assure you, it is much better to have no children than to have them only to give them up! It is too wretched!'

The Great Stink

The year 1858 is remembered for the 'Great Stink'. After the introduction of flushing lavatories at the Great Exhibition, there was a boom in their popularity. But the waste was flushed directly into the Thames. By 1858, the river had grown so rank that the curtains of the Houses of Parliament had to be dipped in lime chloride to mask the stench and enable members to speak without holding handkerchiefs over their noses. Buckingham Palace reeked of excrement. Both the palace and Windsor ran with rodents. Victoria recorded her two little dogs chasing an enormous rat around her bedroom. This ended with one of them, 'Däckel', killing it – 'He behaved most valiantly, but the rat made an awful noise, though he was killed right out pretty quickly.'

Like many sophisticated ladies of the time, Victoria kept a rat or two in a gilded cage. She also employed an official rat catcher called Jack Black, who wore a self-made uniform comprising scarlet topcoat, waistcoat and breeches, with a huge leather sash inset with cast-iron rats.

On Coronation Day, 28 June, Victoria and Albert went to see Isambard Kingdom Brunel's iron sailing ship *Great Eastern*, which was under construction at Millwall Iron Works. They returned by barge and found themselves 'half poisoned by the fearful smell of the Thames'.

Consequently, they stayed away from London, preferring the sweeter air on the Isle of Wight or in the Highlands, where they often lodged in a small wood and granite hut at Glassalt Shiel on Loch Muick near Braemar. There they fished for trout and 'felt so peaceable & happy in this little cottage, far away from all human habitations'.

Illness in the family

In the Highlands, they tried to travel incognito, but were given away by the rings Victoria wore, the crest on their expensive bed sheets and the crown on the dogcart. In October 1859, they climbed Ben Muich Dhui, the second highest peak in Britain. On the trip, they took with them the gillie John Brown.

That year, Victoria's mother fell ill. She wrote to Leopold saying: 'I hardly myself knew how I loved her, or how my whole existence seems bound up with her, till I saw looming in the distance the fearful possibility of what I will not mention.'

The Duchess of Kent finally died on 16 March 1861. Victoria described it as: 'The dreaded terrible calamity has befallen us, which seems like an awful dream, from which I cannot recover.'

Victoria was holding the Duchess's hand as she died and said: 'I, her poor child, have lost the mother I tenderly loved, whom I had never been parted from these 41 years, excepting for a few weeks & 3 times for 3 months!'

She cried inconsolably for weeks and was plunged into depression. The intensity of her grief led to rumours that she had inherited the madness of her grandfather George III. Albert begged her to control her feelings and advised her to take increased interest in things unconnected with them. As it was, she retreated as much as possible to Osborne House or Balmoral and fretted whenever Albert left her. She wrote to Vicky saying that she did not want to be 'roused out of' her grief. Worse. Having lost her half-brother Charles, she fretted over the health of Feodora, now 50, saying: 'May God long preserve this dear & only sister! I tremble so now for all those dear to me!'

In 1860, Victoria was looking for suitors for Alice and bemoaned: 'All marriage is such a lottery – the happiness is always an exchange – though it may be a very happy one – still the poor woman is bodily and morally the husband's slave. That always sticks in my throat.'

She even toyed with the idea of fleeing to Australia with her children.

Chapter Twelve

WIDOWHOOD

Albert had never been physically strong. Stress led to bouts of vomiting, but Victoria often wrote this off as hypochondria. In 1861, she wrote to Vicky: 'Dear Papa never allows he is any better or will try to get over it, but makes such a miserable face that people always think he's very ill. It is quite the contrary with me always; I can do anything before others and never show it, so people never believe I am ill or ever suffer. His nervous system is easily excited and irritated and he's so completely overpowered by everything.'

The bane of Albert's existence was Bertie, who would one day be king – the position Albert had always coveted. The child was a worry from the beginning. As a toddler, he was given to tempestuous tantrums – a trait inherited from his mother. When he was five, she wrote: 'He is a very good child & not at all wanting in intellect, but he is a little awkward & shy & often does not do himself justice.'

He always compared badly to his big sister. When he was eight, a phrenologist was called in. Examining the child's skull, he found an 'inaptitude for mental labour, and an aversion to it at particular times'. The organs of combativeness, destructiveness and firmness were enlarged, while the 'intellectual organs are only moderately developed'.

Albert's greatest fear was that he would become profligate like his Hanoverian uncles, or indeed Albert's own father. As a child, he was regularly whipped – as were his sisters, though less often. Having failed to shine academically, Bertie was sent for infantry training. In the summer of 1861, he was at an army camp at the Curragh, near Dublin, where the actress Nellie Clifden was smuggled into his tent to entertain him. She was indiscreet and the story was soon circulating in the clubs of London. When Albert heard of this assignation, he went to confront Bertie, who had now returned to Cambridge. They went for a long walk together to discuss the matter and got soaked to the skin in a rainstorm.

Broken heart

When Albert returned to the chill of Windsor, he fell ill. Victoria blamed Bertie. Despite his failing health, Albert still did not stop working. On 30 November 1861, Albert wrote one final despatch. An American warship stopped a British mail packet and removed two Confederate envoys, who were bound for England to ask for diplomatic recognition of the Confederacy. Albert's delicate handling of the matter prevented Britain from getting involved in the American Civil War. By 2 December, Albert had retired to bed, liberally dosed with opiates. Five days later he was often incoherent and Victoria said she 'felt as if my heart must break'.

During the day, she kept vigil at his bedside, weeping. They prayed together. Meanwhile, the doctors assured her that he would recover. On the morning of 14 December, she was told that the crisis was over. But when she went to see him, the doctors looked anxious. 'I went in, and never can I forget how beautiful my darling looked, lying there with his face lit up by the rising sun,' she said.

That afternoon in the Blue Room at Windsor Castle, Albert's eyes opened, but he did not move. She kissed him over and over again. His breathing was faint and laboured, his skin was white and his hair was stuck down by sweat. By and by his hand grew colder: 'Oh no,' she said. 'I have seen this before. This is death.'

Then she let out a cry of anguish and dropped to her knees. He was gone. He was only 42 years old. It was not entirely clear what killed him as she would not allow a post mortem, but it is generally thought to have been typhoid from the poor drains of Windsor. However, in Victoria's eyes it was Bertie and Albert's trip to Cambridge to chastise him that were to blame.

That night she had to be sedated with opium. Even so, she cried all night. She had Albert's nightclothes laid out on the bed next to her and Alice stayed with her. Victoria was so upset that she did not attend Albert's funeral. A portrait of her at the age of 24 was put in his coffin. The sculptor Carlo Marochetti was commissioned to make effigies of the couple to place on their tomb in the mausoleum at Frogmore. Every day she was at Windsor, she prayed there, gazing at his likeness. 'My only wish is to follow him soon,' she said. 'To live without him is really no life.'

She decreed that the Court would be in mourning for an unprecedented two years. After that her daughters and the other ladies could go into half-mourning, wearing white, grey or light purple. The Queen herself had dressed in black for nearly ten years by then, due to the deaths of relatives and other dignitaries. She threw off her stays, as there was no one to keep in shape for, and would wear only black for the rest of her life. The children were forbidden laughter or any light-hearted pleasures that might indicate they were not grieving for their father.

That Christmas, everyone in the royal household was given a memento of Albert. The poet laureate Alfred Lord Tennyson was asked to write some lines to mark his passing. She kept casts of his hands and face beside her bed, sometimes clutching the cold stone in hope of comfort. There was a portrait of Albert by his side of the bed and she would hold his dressing gown as she slept. Again, there were fears for her sanity and an appeal was made to the leader of the opposition, Lord Derby, not to try and bring down the government at such a delicate juncture.

Two years after Albert's death, there was speculation that she might abdicate, but Bertie was not popular and it was known that Victoria and others blamed him for his father's death. Victoria refused to let him take over any of Albert's duties, taking on the work herself and praying that she would outlive him.

Fading presence

Without Albert, Victoria withdrew further from public life, refusing to attend the opening of parliament in 1864. She never attended another public ball and Alice's wedding to Prince Louis of Hesse-Darmstadt in July 1862 was as sombre as a funeral. She fought back the tears during the ceremony and skipped the reception. Later, the Queen admonished Alice for spending too much time away from England, though she returned to Windsor to give birth to a daughter, Victoria, the following April.

At the wedding of Bertie to Alexandra of Denmark on 10 March 1863, Victoria sat in a closet high above the altar of St George's Chapel at Windsor. She reached it through a covered walkway through the deanery, as she no longer liked being seen. When the trumpets sounded announcing the entrance of the bride, she recalled her own wedding and almost passed out. Again, she skipped the reception, dining alone with five-year-old Beatrice.

'Here I sit lonely & desolate, who so need love & tenderness, while our 2 daughters have each their loving husbands & Bertie has taken his lovely pure sweet Bride to Osborne, – such a jewel whom he is indeed lucky to have obtained. How I pray God may ever bless them! Oh! what I suffered in the Chapel,' she wrote in her journal.

Alex gave birth to a son, Albert Victor, the following January. Victoria's relationship with Bertie improved after his marriage, but she would still not allow him any official duties.

When Prussia invaded the disputed duchy of Schleswig, loyal to his wife, Bertie urged the British government to intervene on the side of Denmark. He was told to hold his tongue as his brother-in-law, Vicky's husband Fritz, was fighting in the Prussian army. To keep peace in the family, Victoria insisted on neutrality.

Victoria became entrenched in the idea of widowhood. A month after Albert had died, 200 men and boys had died in a mining accident. After a ceremony consecrating Albert's remains, the Duchess of Sutherland gave her a Bible, signed by 'loyal English widows', including those of the men who had died in the disaster. She wrote back:

MY DEAREST DUCHESS: — I am deeply touched by the gift of a Bible 'from many widows,' and by the very kind and affectionate thoughts which accompanied it... Pray express to all these kind sister-widows the deep and heartfelt gratitude of their widowed Queen, who can never feel grateful enough for the universal sympathy she has received, and continues to receive, from her loyal and devoted subjects. But what she values far more is the appreciation of her adored and perfect husband. To her, the only consolation she experiences is in the constant sense of his unseen presence and the blessed thought of the Eternal Union hereafter, which will make the bitter anguish of the present appear as naught. That our

Heavenly Father may impart to 'many widows' those sources of consolation and support, is their broken-hearted Queen's earnest prayer...
Believe me ever yours most affectionately,
VICTORIA

Though her widowhood, she reached out to others, writing: 'I would as soon clasp the poorest widow in the land to my heart, if she had truly loved her husband and felt for me, as I would a Queen or any other high position.'

She asked George Anson's sister Lady Eliza Jane Waterpark to attend her and join 'our sad sisterhood' after her husband died, saying: 'I think that we understand one another, and feel that life is ended for us, except in the sense of duty.'

Then when Abraham Lincoln was assassinated in 1865, Victoria wrote to his widow Mary, saying:

Dear Madam,
Though a Stranger to you I cannot remain silent when so terrible a calamity has fallen upon you & your Country & must personally express my deep & heartfelt sympathy with you under the shocking circumstances of your present dreadful misfortune –
No one can better appreciate than I can, who am myself utterly broken-hearted by the loss of my own beloved Husband, who was the Light of my Life, – my Stay – my all, – what your sufferings must be; and I earnestly pray that you may be supported by Him to whom Alone the sorely stricken can look for comfort, in this hour of heavy affliction.
With the renewed Expression of true sympathy, I remain, dear Madam,

Your Sincere friend
Victoria Rg

Nervous exhaustion

Victoria now stayed away from Buckingham Palace and split her time between Windsor, Osborne and Balmoral. Without Albert, she threw herself back into her work. However, she rejected repeated calls for her to appear in public.

She eventually attended the opening of parliament in February 1866, but even then she wore a veil and used a side entrance to keep her from the gaze of the crowds. Lord John Russell, the prime minister at the time, said it was a 'very severe trial' for her. She told him she was 'terrible shaken, exhausted and unwell from the violent nervous shock of the effort she had made' before making her escape to Osborne.

That ordeal over, she returned to royal duties, even holding Court at Buckingham Palace again. In July 1866, she defied precedence to give away her daughter Helena when she married Prince Christian of Schleswig-Holstein. She opened parliament again in 1887, but for the rest of her reign did this infrequently and always let the Lord Chancellor read the Queen's Speech rather than reading it herself.

As a young queen, Victoria's politics had been decidedly Whig, but her head had been turned somewhat during Albert's lifetime and his political persuasion lay elsewhere. As the Liberal MP William Gladstone put it: 'The Prince is very strongly Conservative in his politics and his influence with the Queen is over-ruling; through him she has become so attached to Conservative ideas that she could hardly endure the idea of the opposite Party as her ministers.' So, she was delighted when Benjamin Disraeli led the

Conservative Party to victory and became prime minister in 1868, and doubly so when he used his skill with words to flatter her and begged for 'the benefit of your Majesty's guidance'.

'The present man will do well,' she remarked to Vicky. 'He is very peculiar, thoroughly Jewish looking... but very clever and sensible... He is full of poetry, romance and chivalry. When he knelt down to kiss my hand, he said: "In loving loyalty and faith."'

After ten months, he was ousted by Gladstone, who Victoria disliked, as she felt he patronized her, once saying that he addressed her as though she was a public meeting. He sought to address the question of Irish home rule, but this did not satisfy the Fenian Brotherhood who wanted full independence. The threat of terrorism meant that soldiers had to be stationed at Osborne, while the Royal Navy patrolled the Solent. Sectarian strife between Irish Catholics and non-Catholics was not confined to Britain. Prince Alfred was on a tour of Australia at the time, and there had been a shooting incident between Orange and Catholic factions in Melbourne. While attending a fundraising picnic in the Sydney suburb of Clontarf, the Prince was shot in the back. The would-be assassin, Henry James O'Farrell, fired from close range but the Prince was only wounded. Despite his history of mental illness, O'Farrell was convicted of attempted murder and hanged at Darlinghurst Gaol.

Awkward allegiances

In the Seven Weeks' War between Prussia and Austria in 1866 – part of Bismarck's campaign to unify Germany – Victoria's children were again to find themselves on opposing sides. Vicky's husband Fritz was with the Prussians and Alice's husband Ludwig with the Austrians, while Alice herself worked as a nurse. So, when looking for a husband for Louise, Victoria abandoned Albert's geopolitical strategy. She wrote to Bertie, saying: 'Times have changed; great foreign alliances are looked on as causes of trouble and anxiety, and are of no good. What could be more painful than the position in which our family was placed during the wars with Denmark, and between Prussia and Austria?'

Louise married John, Marquess of Lorne – later Duke of Argyll. The marriage was childless. It was rumoured that he was homosexual and they drifted apart. An unconventional royal, she became a sculptor.

There were rumours that she had affairs with her fellow artists Joseph Boehm and Edwin Lutyens, among others. The policy of making political marriages resumed in 1866, when Helena married Prince Christian of Schleswig-Holstein – by then the two duchies had been swallowed up by Prussia.

Victoria grew estranged from Alice who urged her to be seen in public more often. She was unable to visit Vicky when she lost a child to meningitis, but became more thoughtful when it came to the haemophiliac Leopold, kissing him every night, and she struggled to compensate for the loss of the children's father. However, when a clergyman wrote saying that 'henceforth Christ himself will be your husband', Victoria commented: 'That is what I call twaddle.'

On 10 December 1865, she suffered by far the heaviest loss since the death of her husband. After many months of painful illness, her ailing Uncle Leopold died, depriving her of a surrogate father and trusted advisor. 'A sad, sad blow, which has long been impending, has at last fallen on us, & I can hardly believe what I write & am stupefied & stunned. Dearly beloved Uncle Leopold is no more, that dear loving Uncle, who has ever been to me a Father, has gone to that everlasting Name, where all is peace and rest,' she wrote.

Now the head of the Saxe-Coburg family, she felt the loneliness of her position. Perhaps in reaching that nadir, she grew accepting: 'The violent grief is past,' she wrote to Lady Waterpark in 1867. 'I almost grieve for that.' However, as the grief lifted, she felt that she was being disloyal to Albert.

As time went by, she began to take a delight in nature again, though there was more grief to come. Lehzen died in 1870, and Feodora two years later. Victoria began to feel her age too, suffering from rheumatism, headaches and toothache.

Chapter Thirteen

FINAL FAVOURITES

On Thursday 3 October 1850, Victoria had been at Balmoral, where she wrote: 'I also like the other gillie, John Brown, very much, a good looking, tall lad of 23, with fair curly hair, so very good humoured & willing, – always ready to do whatever is asked, & always with a smile on his face. – Grant is an excellent simple, plain spoken man & I have a very high opinion of him. He is so much attached to those he serves. I enter into these details to show the people's characters, & our Mode of life amongst them here.'

Since then, Brown had accompanied royal parties in the Highlands. On 7 October 1863, Victoria was returning home late, led by Brown on foot, when the coach overturned and the women were thrown clear. She recorded in her journal: 'I came very hard with my face on the ground, but with a strength I should not have thought myself capable of, I managed to scramble up at once, saw Alice & Lenchen lying on the ground, near the carriage, both the horses on the ground & Brown calling out in despair, "the lord Almighty have mercy on us! Who did ever see the like of this before, I thought you were all killed!"'

Although she nursed a black eye, it was clear that she did not want to die as much as she thought she did. 'Lonely & weary as my life now was I yet realized & felt more & more, how necessary

John Brown (1826–1883), 'personal attendant' to Queen Victoria. She became such close friends with Brown that their relationship created scandal.

I was to my Children & Country & to the carrying out of dearest Albert's wishes & plans,' she said. 'For all this I must try & live on for a while yet! My suffering is as great as ever but there is resignation & submission, which was so hard for me at first.'

Her doctors advised her to ride and in October 1864, she sent for Brown to attend her at Osborne, 'in order to lead my pony, as Dr Jenner is so anxious I should keep up my riding, & I am so accustomed to Brown always leading the pony. A stranger would make me nervous. Sir C. Phipps thinks it a very good idea. Alas! I am now weak & nervous, & very dependent on those I am accustomed to & in whom I have confidence.'

He was given the title the Queen's Highland Servant – known in the household as 'the Queen's Stallion' – then became John Brown Esquire. She wrote: 'He is so devoted to me – so simple, so intelligent, so unlike an ordinary servant, and so cheerful and attentive.'

She travelled with him to London and Scotland, even accompanying her when she visited the Continent. For 18 years, he steered her around the dance floor, rowed her boat, lifted her on to her horse and carried her when she could not walk, admitting unashamedly that he was her best friend. Other courtiers were shocked at his lack of deference. When pinning a tartan shawl on her, the Queen moved and he grazed her with the pin. 'Hoots, woman, canna ye hold yer head still,' he said.

There were long, solitary rides together and attendance in her room. The prime minister said: 'The princesses – perhaps unwisely – make a joke of the matter, and talk of him as "Mamma's lover".'

The Queen overlooked his heavy drinking, as she did that of other servants. Her children did not and they despised him. The public too were suspicious, thinking that he was keeping the Queen in seclusion. Scandal beckoned when Edwin Landseer's official portrait *Her Majesty at Osborne* showed the Queen on horseback with Brown holding the bridle. By 1868, people talked openly of Victoria being 'Mrs Brown'. When the Cabinet sought to prevent him from appearing in public with her, her doctor warned that she might vomit violently or go mad.

The stories of an affair between Victoria and Brown are largely empty speculation. Nonetheless, her children and others went to great lengths to sift through her journals and other written records to weed out mentions of the man. The biographer Julia Baird found in the diaries of Victoria's trusted doctor, Sir James Reid, an entry for 22 March 1883 where he opened the door to Victoria's room to find her flirting with John Brown as she 'walked a little'. Brown said to her, lifting his kilt, 'Oh, I thought it was here?' She responded, lifting her dress, 'No, it is here.' Of course, it is not explicit what 'it' was, but clearly they were more intimate than it was usual for a monarch to be with her subject.

Reid's diaries also recorded that he was despatched in 1905 by Bertie to obtain a cache of some 300 letters in the possession of the son of Alexander Profeit, the manager of Balmoral, who disliked Brown. It is not known how much he paid for them, but they were burned immediately. They were, he noted, 'very compromising'.

On 29 February 1872, 17-year-old Arthur O'Connor climbed the fence of Buckingham Palace. When the Queen returned from a drive, she was about to alight from her carriage when he thrust his face into hers. 'It is difficult for me to describe, as my impression was a great fright, & all was over in a minute,' Victoria recorded. 'How it all happened I knew nothing of. The Equerries had dismounted, Brown had got down, to let down the steps & Jane C. was just getting out, when suddenly someone appeared at my side, whom I at first imagined was a footman, going to lift off the wrapper. Then I perceived that it was someone unknown, peering above the carriage door, with an uplifted hand & a strange voice, at the same time the Boys calling out & moving forward. Involuntarily, in a terrible fright, I threw myself over Jane C., calling out, "save me", & heard a scuffle & voices! I soon recovered myself sufficiently to stand up & turn around, when I saw Brown holding a young man tightly, who was struggling, Arthur, the Equerries &c, also near him. They laid the man on the ground & Brown kept hold of him till several of the Police came in. All turned & asked if I was hurt & I said "not at all". Then Ld Charles Gen: Hardinge, & Arthur came up saying they thought the man had dropped something. We looked, but could find nothing, when Cannon, the Postilion, called out "there it is" & looking down I then did see shining on the ground a small pistol!! This filled us with horror. All were as white as sheets,

Queen Victoria described Balmoral as 'my dear paradise in the Highlands'.

Jane C. almost crying & Leopold looked as if he were going to faint. It is to good Brown & to his wonderful presence of mind, that I greatly owe my safety, for he alone saw the boy rush round & followed him!'

The Times mistakenly reported: 'The Queen showed no sign whatsoever of fear.'

Brown had grabbed the assailant by the throat and forced him to drop the pistol. For this, she created and awarded him the Victoria Devoted Service Medal. On the reverse, it was inscribed: 'To John Brown, Esq., in recognition of his presence of mind and devotion at Buckingham Palace, February 29, 1872'. He seems to have been the only recipient of the honour.

The assailant, Arthur O'Connor, a clerk whose life had been dogged by an accident when he was run down by a cab, seriously injuring his head, was an Englishman but a self-proclaimed Irish Nationalist and the great-nephew of the Chartist leader Feargus O'Connor. His aim was to get Victoria to sign a document freeing and pardoning Fenian prisoners and thereby achieve everlasting fame. The document gave his address in Houndsditch and said that, if he was found guilty of 'having committed an outrage against my Royal person', he was to be shot rather than hanged.

John Brown and Prince Leopold appeared in court as witnesses. O'Connor was found to be insane and sentenced to just one year in prison. Victoria was outraged and wrote to Gladstone, expressing her 'surprise and annoyance at the extreme leniency of O'Connor's sentence, especially as regards the length of the imprisonment… To let this deluded youth out again, in a year, when he has himself only the other day avowed that he would not have minded if he had been torn to pieces, if he had obtained the release of the Prisoners, is most dangerous.'

In fact, in prison, O'Connor was to be birched and put to hard labour despite his poor health. Victoria was adamant that he should not be returned to the streets. Gladstone suggested it might be possible to commute his sentence if he was to leave the country for good. With the birching suspended, O'Connor agreed. On 27 January 1873, he was pardoned and was sent to Australia.

After two months in New South Wales, O'Connor wrote a long, personal – and excruciatingly poetic – letter to the Queen asking her to dismiss Alfred, Lord Tennyson and appoint him poet laureate in Tennyson's place. The letter never reached the Queen. It was intercepted by the home secretary Henry Bruce, who noted: 'The man must be mad; his self-conceit is intolerable.'

He later turned violent again, seriously injuring a policeman and was again declared insane. He would then spend some 50 years in various lunatic asylums.

Brown's heroic action had strengthened the bond between him and Victoria. He stayed with her at the cottage at Glassalt Shiel on the Balmoral estate, which she had had extended since the death of Albert. On her 51st birthday in 1871, despite the presence of Beatrice, Affie and Leopold, she wrote: 'Alone, alone, as it will ever be!' She tried to explain her affection for Brown to Vicky, writing: 'When one's beloved Husband is gone, & one's Children are married – one feels that a friend… who can devote him or herself entirely to you is the one thing you do require to help you on – & to sympathize entirely with you. Not that you love your Children less – but you feel as they grow up & marry that you can be of so little use to them, & they to you (especially in the Higher Classes).'

On New Year's Day 1877, she sent a postcard to Brown with a picture of a chambermaid on the front. She wrote on it: 'To my best friend JB/From his best friend VRI' – she was now Empress of India.

The message read:

> *I send my sewing maiden*
> *With New Year letter laden,*
> *Its words will prove*
> *My faith and love*
> *To you my heart's best treasure,*
> *Then smile on her and smile on me*
> *And let your answer loving be,*
> *And give me pleasure.*

Victoria was soon to lose another favourite. Disraeli was ousted from power once again by Gladstone in 1880, much to Victoria's dismay. The following spring, as he lay dying, he was asked whether the Queen should visit: 'No, it is better not,' he replied. 'She would only ask me to take a message to Albert.'

She sent a bunch of primroses to his funeral. The accompanying card said they were 'his favourite flowers from Osborne'.

Queen Victoria was shot at again in 1882 after she got off the train at Windsor by another would-be poet named Roderick Maclean. She was beginning to get blasé about it. 'It is worth being shot at,' said Victoria, 'to see how much one is loved.'

Brown was with her again.

'At 4.30. left Buckingham Palace for Windsor,' said Victoria. 'Just as we were driving off from the station there, the people or rather, the Eton Boys cheered, & at the same time there was the sound, of what I thought, was an explosion from the engine, but in another moment, I saw people rushing about, & a man being violently hustled, people rushing down the street. I then realised that it was a shot, which must have been meant for me, though I was not sure, & Beatrice said nothing, the Duchess, who was also

THE ILLUSTRATED LONDON NEWS

REGISTERED AT THE GENERAL POST-OFFICE FOR TRANSMISSION ABROAD.

No. 2256.—VOL. LXXX.   SATURDAY, MARCH 11, 1882.   WITH TWO SUPPLEMENTS   SIXPENCE By Post, 6½d.

THE PRISONER

THE PISTOL

CARTRIDGE

THE BULLET ON LARGER SCALE

ATTEMPT TO SHOOT THE QUEEN AT THE WINDSOR RAILWAY STATION.—SEE PAGE 228.
FROM A SKETCH SUPPLIED BY MR. BURNSIDE, PHOTOGRAPHER.

The front page of The Illustrated London News *after Roderick Maclean attempted to shoot Queen Victoria at Windsor railway station on 4 March 1882.*

in the carriage, thinking it was a joke. No one gave me a sign to lead me to believe, anything amiss had happened, Brown, however, when he opened the carriage, said, with a greatly perturbed face, though quite calm: "that man fired at Yr Majesty's carriage."'

Maclean was arrested and charged with high treason. He was found 'not guilty but insane'. This prompted Victoria to ask for a change in the law. The Trial of Lunatics Act of 1883 changed the wording of the verdict to 'guilty but insane'. The change meant little to Maclean who died in Broadmoor in 1921.

In early March 1883, Brown was busy scouring the grounds around Windsor Castle for suspected Fenians. A few days later his duties switched to carrying around the Queen who had sprained her knee after falling down stairs. Shortly after that, he came down with erysipelas, an infection that causes a painful swelling of the skin. On 27 March, he died, aged 56.

Writing to his sister-in-law, Victoria said: 'He was the best, the truest heart that ever beat.' Again, she was inconsolable, saying her grief was 'unbounded, dreadful & I know not how to bear it'.

He was buried alongside his parents in Crathie Kirkyard. The inscription on his gravestone read:

*This stone is erected in affectionate and grateful
remembrance of John Brown the devoted and faithful
personal attendant and beloved friend of Queen Victoria
in whose service he had been for 34 years.*

*Born at Crathienaird 8th Decr. 1826 died at
Windsor Castle 27th March 1883.*

*That Friend on whose fidelity you count
that Friend given to you by circumstances
over which you have no control was God's own gift.*

Well done good and faithful servant
Thou hast been faithful over a few things,
I will make thee ruler over many things.
Enter through into the joy of the Lord.

The Queen also commissioned a life-sized statue of Brown by Edgar Boehm shortly after his death, which stood outside Balmoral. The inscription read: 'Friend more than Servant. Loyal. Truthful. Brave. Self less than Duty, even to the Grave.'

She compared his loss to the loss of Albert and it hit her as hard. Her private secretary Henry Ponsonby recorded: 'The Queen is trying hard to occupy herself but she is utterly crushed & her life has again sustained one of those shocks like in 61 when every link has been shaken & torn & at every turn & every moment the loss of the strong arm & wise advice, warm heart & cheery original way of saying things & the sympathy in any large & small circumstances – is most cruelly missed.'

Again, she sought comfort from Tennyson, saying of Brown: 'He had no thought but for me, my welfare, my comfort, my safety, my happiness. Courageous, unselfish, totally disinterested, discreet to the highest degree, speaking the truth fearlessly and telling me what he thought and considered to be "just and right," without flattery and without saying what would be pleasing if he did not think it right... The comfort of my daily life is gone – the void is terrible – the loss is irreparable!'

She dedicated *More Leaves from the Journal of a Life in the Highlands* to Brown and wrote a memoir of him, which she had to be discouraged from publishing. The manuscript was destroyed along with Brown's diaries when Edward VII became king.

After her fall, Victoria could no longer walk without the support of two sticks. She had to be hauled from her carriage to the train in a special chair and carried upstairs.

When Gladstone was toppled in 1885, Lord Salisbury took over. He was the first of her prime ministers to be younger than her. They got on well and she fought tooth and nail to try to prevent Gladstone from returning to power. Gladstone and Salisbury would practically alternate in office for the rest of the century. When she finally rid herself of Gladstone in 1894, Victoria wrote to him saying, cruelly, that she 'would gladly have offered a peerage of Mr Gladstone, but she knows he would not accept it'. Gladstone complained that he had been dismissed like a tradesman. Lord Rosebery served briefly as prime minister before Salisbury resumed the position once more.

In 1887, Victoria decided to mark her Golden Jubilee by employing some Indian staff – after all she had been their Empress for more than ten years. One of them was a 24-year-old clerk from Agra named Abdul Karim, who was accompanied by Mohammed Buksh. They kissed her feet in deference and went to work for the 68-year-old queen.

The following year, she wrote that she was 'making arrangements to appoint Abdul a Munshi' – that is, a clerk. 'I think it was a mistake to bring him over as a servant to wait at table, a thing he had never done, having been a clerk or *munshi* in his own country & being of rather a different class to the others,' she said. They grew close and he told her of the country's history and culture, and taught her Hindustani and Urdu.

The royal household were outraged when she gave him a bungalow at Windsor and cottages at Balmoral and Osborne, along with a tract of land in Agra. He was also made a Companion of the Most Eminent Order of the Indian Empire and she had his portrait painted with a background of gold. She fussed over his care and, when he fell ill, she would visit him in his room and stroke his hand. In October 1889, she took him to Glassalt Shiel, giving him John Brown's old room, despite having sworn she would never stay there again after Brown's death. Karim also took over Brown's task of carrying her when she could not walk.

When a jewelled brooch went missing, it was discovered that Karim's brother-in-law, Hourmet Ali, had sold it to a jeweller in Windsor. Instead of prosecuting Ali, she railed at her dresser who had lost it and the jeweller who had reported it. Karim explained that it was Indian custom to pick up loose objects without saying anything. Victoria believed him and drew a line under the matter; other members of the household thought Ali had stolen it. Dr Reid wrote: 'So the theft, though proved absolutely, was ignored and even made a virtue of for the sake of [Karim] about whom the Queen seems off her head.'

In 1893, Karim went back to India to fetch his wife and her mother. Victoria went to Frogmore Cottage to see them. 'The Munshi's wife wore a beautiful sari of crimson gauze,' she wrote. 'She is nice looking, but would not raise her eyes, she was so shy.'

Other members of the royal family accompanied Victoria on her visits. Two more wives, who Karim described as 'aunts', followed. Dr Reid discovered that Karim had gonorrhoea. The Queen was shocked, but it made no difference to her affection for him.

Karim was very aware of his status. He walked out of a concert at Sandringham when he was seated next to the servants. After a similar incident in Coburg, at the wedding of two of Victoria's grandchildren, his letter of complaint to her was so strident that she burst into tears. From them on, he was driven around Albert's hometown in a royal carriage. In the royal train, he insisted on sitting with the men of the household and at the races he mixed with the gentry. On a trip to Italy, he complained that the Italian

A vintage illustration of Queen Victoria with Abdul Karim, listening to a despatch from her troops during the Boer War.

newspapers took too little notice of him. The Queen said she would have a word with the editors. Others resented this and it outraged Bertie, though he did not have the courage to take the matter up with his mother.

Despite this, everyone saw that his companionship was doing her good. She took a delight in the beauty of nature once more and enjoyed a massage, morning and evening. Karim and Buksh were also enthusiastic participants in the *tableaux vivants* put on to entertain the Queen.

Four men of the Court investigated Karim's background after he had claimed his father was the surgeon general of the British army in India and Dr Reid discovered he was only a lowly pharmacist who worked in an Agra jail. Victoria dismissed their report on his lowly roots as snobbery. 'To make out that the poor good Munshi is so low is really outrageous & in a country like England quite out of place,' she railed, saying she had known archbishops who were sons of a butcher and a grocer. 'Abdul feels cut to the heart to be thus spoken of. The Queen is so sorry for the poor Munshi's sensitive feelings.'

She suspected that the Court's attitude to Karim was pure racism and she would have none of it. On the other hand, when travelling in Italy in 1894, he would not allow other Indians in the same railway carriage as him. Nevertheless, the attacks on him drew them closer together.

Ponsonby feared that it was dangerous for Karim to see every confidential paper on the subject of India, though he considered him too stupid and uneducated to be a spy, saying that 'his one idea in life seems to be to do nothing & to eat as much as he can'. While Ponsonby thought Karim dim, he was worried about his association with Rafiuddin Ahmed, a political activist involved with the Muslim Patriotic League in London. There were suspicions that Ahmed was milking state secrets from Karim and passing them on to Britain's enemies in Afghanistan.

In 1897, there was a rebellion in the royal household when the Queen announced her intention of taking Karim on holiday with her to the south of France. They informed her that their collective decision was to resign if he did so. Victoria was furious, the household backed down and the Queen got her way. The same thing happened again in 1898, but Victoria's new private secretary, Arthur Bigge, prevented him from bringing Ahmed too.

Allegations began to surface that Karim too was mixed up in the Muslim Patriotic League and he was then accused of stealing money from the Queen. Dr Reid let her know that he had been 'questioned as to her sanity'. But Victoria continued to defend Karim, even when a picture of them at work together appeared in the *Daily Graphic* at his insistence, a glaring breach of protocol. Again, she blamed 'my Gentlemen wishing to spy upon and interfere with one of my people whom I have no personal reason or proof of doubting'.

When Bertie succeeded his mother, the new king had all Karim's papers burnt. After the funeral, he was ordered to leave for India. Detectives were sent to make sure he had taken no papers with him. Back in Agra, Karim lived contentedly on the land Victoria had procured for him and died in 1909 at the age of 46.

Chapter Fourteen

THE GRANDMOTHER OF EUROPE

In 1876, Queen Victoria reached what for many was the zenith of her reign when the prime minister Benjamin Disraeli declared a change of title for the sovereign, adding Empress of India to her role as Queen of the United Kingdom of Great Britain and Ireland. Although India had been under crown control since 1858, this new title was a gesture to further link the monarch with the empire and bind India more closely to Britain. The Queen was flattered and extremely pleased. As well as her belief that the sovereign should have an important and active role in politics, she also felt she had a special part to play in foreign affairs.

Though limited by British constitutional arrangements, Victoria's influence cannot be underestimated. At its height, the British Empire covered over 14 million square miles of territory in which over 450 million people – more than a quarter of the world's population – lived. It encompassed Canada, Australia, some parts of Africa and the South Pacific. But with India as the 'jewel in the crown', the British Empire was no longer just big; it was immense. The Queen was emblematic of the time: an enthusiastic supporter of an empire, on which it was said: 'The sun never sets.'

It was perhaps because of the idea of empire and his assertive foreign policy that Victoria got on so well with Disraeli. His purchase of the Suez Canal in 1875, her new royal title the following year and his triumph at the Congress of Berlin in 1878 that dealt a blow to Russian influence in the Balkans rekindled her interest in world affairs, helping restore public confidence following her long seclusion after the death of her husband Albert.

In Europe, her influence was at its strongest. Either directly, or by the marriages of her children, Victoria was related to the royal houses of nearly every major European power with the exceptions of France and Spain. She ruled over her family with

Members of the royal family at Coburg, Germany, April 1894: the Duke of Connaught, the Duke of Saxe-Coburg and Gotha, Queen Victoria, the German Emperor Wilhelm II, the Empress Friedrich and the Prince of Wales.

an iron hand, and was able to steer her way through most potential conflicts using that familial power. However, family matters were complicated. Victoria's children were at war with each other once again in the Franco-Prussian War of 1870, which France declared for fear of Prussian expansionism. Despite the situation, Victoria agreed to supply arms and horses to France. France lost the war and, as a result, Germany was unified under Wilhelm I of Prussia, Vicky's father-in-law. France became a republic once more and Napoleon III and the Empress Eugénie went into exile in England. Queen Victoria visited them at Camden Place in Chislehurst where they were staying.

As her heir, Bertie continued to be a disappointment to the Queen, taking numerous mistresses even after his marriage to Alexandra of Denmark in 1863. When the husband of one of his alleged co-respondents, Harriet Mordaunt, sued for divorce, Bertie was called as a witness. However, Harriet was conveniently found insane and the case dismissed.

Alfred, who in accordance with his own wishes, had joined the Royal Navy, also drank heavily and took a mistress when posted to Malta. As Duke of Edinburgh, he married the Grand Duchess Maria Alexandrovna, the second daughter of Tsar Alexander II of Russia, in St Petersburg. It was the first of her children's weddings Victoria had missed. Because of his condition, Leopold was cosseted at home, though he was awarded honorary commands in the British army. As Duke of Albany, he married Princess Helena of Waldeck and Pyrmont. Arthur became a soldier, married Princess Louise Margaret of Prussia and went on to become governor-general of Canada.

In 1871, Victoria fell ill. She was still recovering when Bertie came down with a fever. She travelled to Sandringham to visit him three times, each time expecting to find him dead. When he,

*Queen Victoria with her great-grandson Prince Edward of York,
later King Edward VIII.*

too, recovered, there was a thanksgiving service at St Paul's and Victoria thought that God had spared him 'to enable him to lead a new life'.

Alice's son Fritz, another haemophiliac, died after a fall in 1873. Three years later Helena's son Harald died of convulsions when just eight days old. He was buried in the vault of St George's Chapel at Windsor and Victoria carried a locket containing strands of the child's hair around her neck.

After a holiday for the whole family in Eastbourne in the summer of 1878, there was more grief to come. Alice's daughter Marie died of diphtheria at the age of four. Alice herself succumbed on 14 December, the 17th anniversary of Albert's death. She was the first of Victoria's children to die during her lifetime. She was just 35.

Hearing the news, Victoria said: 'That this dear, talented, distinguished, tender hearted, noble minded, sweet child, who behaved so admirably, during her dear Father's illness, & afterwards, in supporting me, & helping me in every possible way, – should be called back to her Father, on this very anniversary, seems almost incredible, & most mysterious!'

Vicky's youngest son Waldemar died of diphtheria four months later, but Victoria discouraged further visits home.

Leopold fell down in Cannes in 1884 and died of a brain haemorrhage. He had had a miserable life. She had considered him 'very ugly' and she was frustratingly protective. But she let John Brown bully him.

Victoria tried to keep Beatrice at home too, saying: 'She is the last one I have and I could not live without her.' The Queen made sure that her youngest daughter was never left alone with a man and danced only with her brothers. However, at the age of 27 she fell in love with Prince Henry of Battenberg, known affectionately as Liko. For seven months, their relationship remained secret. Eventually Bertie, Henry's brother Prince Louis of Battenberg and the Queen's son-in-law Grand Duke Louis of Hesse came to plead Beatrice's case. Victoria only gave her approval to their union on condition that they lived with her.

The night before the wedding Victoria hugged her daughter and cried, but she lent Beatrice her own veil for the wedding. After a short honeymoon, Beatrice remained at the Queen's side, while her husband sought adventure abroad. This suited Victoria, though she liked Liko. When her son-in-law visited, he was even allowed to smoke after dinner.

One of their sons, also named Leopold, was a haemophiliac and died at the age of 32 after service in the First World War. Their daughter, Victoria Eugénie, became queen of Spain and passed the gene on to the Spanish royal family.

At Victoria's Golden Jubilee in 1887, held to mark the 50th year of her reign, ranks of royal men walked before her in a procession through the streets of London. They included three sons, five sons-in-law and nine grandsons. Other royals packed the state carriages. There were 43 family members at Westminster Abbey. But while her royal offspring were decked out in glitter and finery, Victoria wore a plain black dress and a bonnet rather than a crown. Her one concession was that the bonnet was trimmed with white lace and rimmed with diamonds. It soon became the fashion. The huge crowds were provided with terraced benching along the ten-mile route and cheered loudly as the gilded state landau, drawn by six cream-coloured horses and accompanied by Indian cavalry, passed by.

Her journals contain long lists of all those lunching and dining at Buckingham Palace to mark the occasion, including 50 foreign kings and princes, along with the governing heads of Britain's overseas colonies and dominions. Nevertheless, on the eve of the Jubilee, she noted: 'The day has come, & I am alone, though surrounded by many dear Children.'

Clearly, she was still missing Albert. In a letter to her subjects, thanking the crowds for turning out, she wrote: 'It has shown that the labour and anxiety of fifty long years, twenty-two of which I spent in unclouded happiness, shared and cheered by my beloved husband, while an equal number were full of sorrows and trials, borne without his sheltering arm and wise help, have been appreciated by my people.'

In an effort to present the Queen with a permanent memorial of the Jubilee, campaigners began asking the women and girls of the United Kingdom to raise the money for such an offering as a token of their loyalty and affection for 'the only female sovereign in history who, for fifty years, has borne the toils and troubles of public life, known the sorrows that fall to all women, and as wife, mother, widow and ruler held up a right and spotless example to her own and all other nations'. Three million women raised £75,000 and Victoria commissioned a replica of Baron Marochetti's Glasgow statue of Prince Albert, to be placed in Windsor Great Park. Relaxing Albert's strictures, she allowed women thought to be the innocent parties in divorce cases to attend the Jubilee, but when she thought of extending this to foreigners, Lord Salisbury warned that it risked admitting American women of 'light character'.

Her seven surviving children gathered in London to celebrate her 50 years on the throne. Beatrice, then 30, was pregnant with her second child. The baby girl, Victoria Eugénie, was born four months later and dubbed by her father the 'Jubilee grandchild'. From her studio in Kensington Palace, Louise, 39, was exhibiting at the Royal Academy, the Society of Painters in Watercolour and the Grosvenor Gallery. Helena, 41, was involved in charity work, particularly nursing, and living at Frogmore with her husband. Arthur, 37, was commander in chief of the army in Bombay, while Affie, 42, was commander in chief of the British fleet in the Mediterranean. Bertie, at 45, was still enjoying the high life. The Queen had grown fonder of him, though there were still scandals to come. And Vicky, 46, enjoyed a brief respite from Prussia where she was unpopular, as Germany had turned anti-British. Her son Wilhelm had also grown to hate her. The Queen did not want to invite him to the Jubilee, but Vicky insisted. Wilhelm did at least have the courtesy to wear a British uniform when he visited his grandmother.

Vicky's husband Fritz already had cancer of the throat and could not speak when he became German Emperor Friedrich III in March 1888. Supported by two of his siblings, the conservative Wilhelm had already sought to oust his father from the succession because of his liberal views. Victoria sought to intervene. After holidaying in Italy, she visited Fritz in Prussia. She also had a one-to-one interview with Bismarck, who mopped his brow after the encounter. Victoria also sought to avert her granddaughter Viktoria's marriage to Prince Alexander of Battenberg, who had recently stood down from the throne of Bulgaria. He went on to marry an actress.

After 99 days on the throne, Fritz died. Wilhelm immediately ransacked Vicky's room, looking for documents that might be useful to the British. He fell out with Bertie at Fritz's funeral. Nevertheless, Victoria allowed him to visit her at Osborne in 1889. Again, he wore a British uniform, this time that of an admiral.

With her offspring populating the royal courts of the Continent, Victoria had become known as the 'Grandmother of Europe'. But tragedy still dogged her. In January 1892, Bertie's eldest,

Albert Victor, also known as Prince Eddy, died of pneumonia. Rumours abounded about him. It was said that he was a client of a homosexual brothel in London's Cleveland Street, the father of an illegitimate child with a woman in Whitechapel and even that he was Jack the Ripper.

Alice's daughter, Princess Alix of Hesse, had rejected Prince Eddy, going on to marry Tsar Nicholas II of Russia and perishing in the Russian Revolution. Instead Eddy was due to marry another cousin, Princess Mary of Teck. When he died, she married his younger brother George, who went on to become George V.

By 1895, the relationship between Beatrice and her husband had cooled. Liko had grown close to her sister, the famous beauty Louise, who was known for her many affairs. Louise was then accused of having an affair with the Queen's private secretary Arthur Bigge and her husband, Lord Lorne, was forced to come to her defence. Tired of the squabbling, Liko asked to go on the Ashanti mission, Britain's fourth attempt to annex the Gold Coast, now Ghana. He contracted malaria on the trip and died.

Victoria was desolate now that her favourite daughter Beatrice was suffering the same grief as she had at a similar age. Things were made worse when Louise admitted to being Liko's confidante, revealing that Beatrice had meant no more to him than a shrug of the shoulders. Once more, for Beatrice, there would be no respite from the stifling demands of her mother. Indeed, for 30 years after Victoria's death, Beatrice would be editing – or rather censoring – her mother's diaries.

On Tuesday 22 June 1897, Queen Victoria celebrated her Diamond Jubilee in honour of her 60 years as sovereign. A number of things had changed in the decade since her Golden Jubilee. The Queen was less robust and not particularly keen on yet another expensive celebration, particularly as Britain's economic outlook was less certain. The celebrations were the subject of tense negotiations between the royal household, keen to avoid the expenses incurred by the Golden Jubilee, and the government, who Victoria favoured as the bill payer. In the end, costs were shared between the two and among a number of high-profile philanthropists. Tea magnate Sir Thomas Lipton sponsored tea parties for 400,000 of London's poorest residents, which included free ale and pipe tobacco. Similar events were held in Manchester, Nottingham, Bradford, Hull and other major cities.

Victoria herself took part in a procession from Buckingham Palace, over Westminster Bridge before re-crossing the Thames and making for St Paul's Cathedral for an open-air service, as she was unable to step out of her carriage. She was accompanied by the British Army, the Royal Navy and colonial forces from Canada, India, Africa and the Antipodes. Hundreds of thousands of her subjects lined the route. 'No one ever, I believe, has met with such an ovation as was given to me, passing through those six miles of streets... The crowds were quite indescribable and their enthusiasm truly marvellous and deeply touching,' she recorded later in her journal.

A little girl cried: 'Look! There's Queen Victoria going to heaven' when she saw a large balloon marked 'VICTORIA' floating skyward. The Queen promptly burst into tears and had to be comforted by Bertie's wife Alex.

That year, Uncle Leopold's son and successor, Leopold II, visited her at Balmoral. She recalled: 'He can only shake hands with two fingers as his nails are so long that he dares not run the risk of injuring them. He is an unctuous old monster, very wicked, I believe. We imagine he thinks a visit to the Queen gives him a fresh coat of whitewash, otherwise why does he travel five hundred miles in order to partake of lunch.'

Queen Victoria's carriage passes London Bridge station during her Diamond Jubilee celebrations.

Indeed, he was horribly ugly and 'very wicked'. He was said to have paid to have English virgins sent over to Belgium for his pleasure and was also involved in a brothel that Bertie frequented. What he is now remembered for is the deaths of some 15 million Africans, who perished because of his attempts to establish Belgium as an imperial power. He led the first European efforts to develop the Congo River basin, making possible the formation in 1885 of the Congo Free State, annexed in 1908 as the Belgian Congo. Although he played a significant role in the development of the modern Belgian state, he was also responsible for widespread atrocities committed under his rule.

After the Diamond Jubilee, Vicky was diagnosed with breast cancer. She outlived her mother by just six months. However, she and her six remaining siblings were present for the celebrations marking Victoria's 60-year reign, along with the widowed spouses of Alice and Leopold – Prince Louis of Hesse and Princess Helena of Waldeck and Pyrmont.

At 55, Bertie was still mourning the loss of Eddy and had been caught in another scandal when called as a witness after a friend was accused of cheating at cards. Alfred, at 52, was bored with Coburg and had taken to drink. He was devastated when his only son, the Hereditary Prince Alfred, shot himself following a scandal involving his mistress. He was buried on 10 February, Victoria's wedding anniversary. When his father died of throat cancer, Victoria said she cried out: 'Oh! God! my poor darling Affie gone too! My 3rd grown up child, besides 3 very dear sons-in-law. It is hard at 81!'

Mother-of-four Helena was 51 and still involved in nursing. She had lost two babies – one stillborn, another died when eight days old. Her husband, Prince Christian of Schleswig-Holstein, had lost an eye when he had been accidently shot by his brother-in-law Arthur while out hunting.

Arthur, 47, was the home commander of the British army and happily married with three children. Louise, 49, and her husband hosted a fancy-dress ball at Devonshire House on the night of the Jubilee.

Victoria's last years were dominated by the Second Boer War, which began in October 1899. The sufferings of her soldiers in South Africa roused the 80-year-old queen who undertook a demanding schedule of troop inspections, medal ceremonies and visits to military hospitals to give hope to the wounded and dying. Her initial enthusiasm for the war, against Boers who had been attacking British forces in Natal and Cape Colony, began to wane in the face of casualty lists and news of military defeats. A huge expeditionary force, prepared and sent to the area in late 1900 under the command of Lord Roberts and General Kitchener, eventually turned the tide. The war ended in victory for the British forces, but at the cost of some 100,000 lives and a staggering £250 million [over £20 billion/$26bn at today's prices].

In 1900, protesting against the Boer War, a young Italian tried to kill Bertie and Alex on a train in Brussels. Helena's eldest son and one of Victoria's favourite grandchildren, Prince Christian Victor, had made a career in the British army. He had fought under Kitchener in the Sudan, served on the Ashanti expedition and been at the relief of Ladysmith. While in South Africa, he came down with malaria and died of enteric fever in October 1900, aged 33.

Already bowed by the despatches she read from the war, Christian's death left Victoria shattered. She cried constantly, refused to eat and had to be dosed with opium to sleep. Nevertheless, she travelled to Osborne for the traditional family Christmas. On Christmas eve, Lady Jane Churchill, who had been with Victoria for half a century, died: 'They had not dared tell me for fear of giving me a shock, so had prepared me gradually for the terrible

Albert Edward Prince of Wales (1841–1910), eldest son of Queen Victoria and Prince Albert and later King Edward VII.

news,' wrote Victoria. Her own health began to deteriorate. On 1 January, she wrote: 'Another year begun, – I am feeling so weak & unwell, that I enter upon it sadly.'

On Sunday 13 January 1901, she wrote: 'Had a fair night, but was a little wakeful. Got up earlier & had some milk. – Lenchen came & read some papers. – Out before 1, in the garden chair, Lenchen & Beatrice going with me. – Rested a little, had some food, & took a short drive with Lenchen & Beatrice. – Rested when I came in & at 5.30, went down to the Drawing-room, where a short service was held, by Mr Clement Smith, who performed it so well, & it was a great comfort to me. – Rested again afterwards, then did some signing & dictated to Lenchen.'

It was the last entry she would make in her journal.

By the middle of the month, she was confined to her bed. Bertie and Alex sat up all night with her. On 18 January, she told Dr Reid that she did not want to see Bertie again, in case he tried to get her to alter the arrangements she had made.

The following day Arthur set off from Germany. He was accompanied by Kaiser Wilhelm, even though he had expressed support for the Boers.

On 21 January, Victoria revived a little, telling Reid: 'I should like to live a little longer.'

Back in 1875, she had left instructions that no one but John Brown should watch over her as she died. That duty now fell to Reid, who allowed the Kaiser to see his grandmother alone.

At 4.00 p.m. on 22 January, a bulletin was issued, saying: 'The Queen is slowly sinking.'

At the last moment, Victoria relented and asked Bertie to kiss her face. Dr Reid and Wilhelm stood either side of her. Helena, Louise, Beatrice and Alex were also in attendance. The local vicar and a bishop recited verses from the Bible and prayed until they were hoarse. While Bertie sat with his head in his hands, Reid and Wilhelm raised her up a little. A look of calmness came over her face and she died in the arms of her doctor and her grandson at around 6.30 p.m.

'When it was all over most of the family shook hands with me and thanked me by the bedside,' Reid recorded, 'and the Kaiser also squeezed my hand in silence. I told the Prince of Wales to close her eyes. Later the Prince said: "You are an honest and straightforward Scotchman", and "I shall never forget all you did for the Queen". The Princess [of Wales] cried very much, shook hands and thanked me... I left the dinner table to help the maids and nurse to arrange the Queen's body.'

Three years before she died, Victoria had dictated instructions to be opened only on her death. These were passed to Dr Reid. She included a long list of the things she wanted with her in her coffin. There were the rings from Albert, her mother, Feodora, Louise, Beatrice and John Brown's mother's ring. Then there were the photographs of Albert, and of Brown, along with locks of his hair, one of Brown's handkerchiefs and one of Albert's, along with Albert's cloak and dressing gown, and the shawl made by Alice.

The Queen's own hair was cut off and Dr Reid, Bertie and the Kaiser lifted her body into the coffin. The Order of the Garter was placed across her chest. Her face was covered with a veil and framed with white flowers. The casket was then packed with charcoal and the lid was screwed down.

Victoria's private life was now over as news of the death of the woman who had ruled a quarter of the globe was splashed in newspapers around the world.

Her body would now make the very public journey under guard to the Royal Yacht *Alberta*, which carried her coffin across the Solent, escorted by the larger Royal Yacht *Victoria and Albert*, carrying Bertie, the Kaiser on his own Imperial Yacht SMY *Hohenzollern II*, members of the government on board the *Scott* and two rows of warships drawn up as a guard of honour stretching from Cowes to Portsmouth. These were not just British ships; the battleship *Hatsuse* had been sent by the Emperor of Japan. From midday on, 80 one-minute salvos were fired, the first coming from HMS *Australia*.

Chopin's 'Funeral March' rang out across the water as the *Alberta* slipped into Portsmouth harbour. Two hundred seamen from HMS *Excellent* and 400 Royal Marines formed a guard of honour on the pier, along with naval pensioners, while thousands

The royal mausoleum at Frogmore where Victoria was buried alongside Albert.

looked on. The body was then carried by train from Portsmouth to London Victoria and through the crowds of the capital.

The coffin was then convened on a gun carriage pulled by eight cream horses across town to Paddington, escorted by 700 sailors and Marines, and the Royal Marine Band. Another train carried it on to Windsor, where more crowds and honour guards waited, until she finally rejoined Albert in the royal mausoleum in a tomb she had built for the two of them nearly four decades before.

Despite the fact that the Queen appeared as a frail, 81-year-old lady, the newspapers and magazines of the time printed circulars sent out by the royal household that had been sparing in the details of the last few weeks of her life and consequently her death came as a shock. The country, literally, came to a standstill. People wept openly in the streets, all adults dressed in black and purple banners were hung from shop windows. Theatrical performances were cancelled and the mood all over the country was sombre. There were few dissenting voices. Victoria had reigned for 63 years, at the time the longest in British history, and most British subjects had known no other monarch.

The Britain she left behind at her death was a very different place than when her reign began. She had presided over a period of unprecedented development in industry and science – innovations including the railways, steam-powered ships, gas lighting, the telephone and major advances in manufacturing methods had brought life into a completely new era. Of course, all these things were exported across the empire, which at its peak encompassed a quarter of the world. For the British people, the ever-present Queen Victoria had come to symbolize self-confidence, not just because they belonged to a colonial power, but also because as such they believed they were bringing 'civilization' to the dark corners of the world. The sense of loss at her death was palpable and marked throughout the empire with a deep and heartfelt sorrow.

Victoria's character has come to embody the age that now bears her name. It was an era that idealized motherhood and the family, which she undertook as a duty nine times, despite despising pregnancy and hating young babies. She was not particularly interested in mechanical or technical innovation, yet the 19th century saw huge advances in both; she had little interest in social issues but presided over an age of great reform. But perhaps it is by how much she improved the standing of the monarchy that a measure of her reign can be taken. She came to the throne, aged 18, and with poor royal precedent, following a series of dull, distant and rather badly behaved Hanoverian kings. Previous queens too, although all in the dim and distant past, had poor reputations: Elizabeth was a bit of a tyrant, Mary untrustworthy and Anne too easily influenced by others.

By contrast, Victoria was earnest, steadfast and ever reliable. Politically astute, in an age when men thought politics their own private business, Victoria was determined to retain political power. When she ascended to the throne, the political role of the crown was not clear, nor was the permanence of the throne secure. But through the dignity of her sovereignty and the pragmatism of her political outlook, she secured the monarchy's future, albeit as a ceremonial political institution.

A contemporary article in the *Economist* of December 1901 explained it thus: 'Queen Victoria stands out alone without a blemish as a Sovereign, without a disqualification for reigning, the only one whom, for the last thirty years of her life, her millions of subjects, the conquerors and the conquered alike, would have chosen by plebiscite to occupy the throne… They will never see such a Sovereign again, and it is not a reign, but an era, which closes with her life.'

For Britain, the Boer War marked the beginning of the end of the great imperial dream and the fact that Victoria died as the conflict was approaching its end was highly symbolic. It was as if the sun was just starting to set on the British Empire.

INDEX

Abercromby, James 35
Adelaide of Saxe-Meiningen, Queen 15, 28, 37, 38, 77, 120
Adolphus, Prince 15, 18
Ahmed, Rafiuddin 167–8
Albert, Duke of Connaught 9
Albert, Prince
  and Victoria's funeral 9
  first meetings with Victoria 30–1
  Victoria decides to marry 65–9
  love for Victoria 69–72
  negotiations over position 72–4
  wedding day 74–9
  early married life 81–2
  role after marriage 82–4, 86–7, 91–3, 99–101, 124, 131–2
  assassination attempt on Victoria 84–6
  birth of daughter Victoria 87–8
  relationship with daughter Victoria 90
  control of life in Buckingham Palace 91–2
  sacking of Louise Lehzen 94, 95–7, 99
  becomes Prince Consort 101
  birth of Alice 103
  death of father 104
  first separation from Victoria 105–6
  improvements to royal residences 106, 108
  involvement with children 111–12, 134
  at Balmoral 112–15
  and Great Exhibition 122, 124
  Victoria's outbursts at 124–6
  and Crimean War 131
  celebrates 35th birthday 132–3
  concerns over young Edward VII 143–4
  death of 144–6
  and Golden Jubilee celebrations 175
Albert Victor, Prince (Eddy) 147, 176–7
Alexander, Tsarevich 61
Alexander II, Tsar 171
Alexander of Battenberg, Prince 176
Alexandra of Denmark, Queen 146, 178, 181, 183
Alexandrovna, Maria 171
Alfred, Duke of Saxe-Coburg and Gotha
  birth of 106
  assassination attempt on 150
  work and marriage 171, 176
  death of 180
Ali, Hourmet 165
Alice, Princess
  birth of 103
  death of Albert 145
  marriage to Prince Louis 146
  death of 173
Alix of Hesse, Princess 177
Anne, Queen 13
Anson, George 73, 88, 92, 120
Arthur, Prince 120, 157, 171, 176, 181

Augusta of Hesse-Cassel, Princess 15, 18
Augustus, Duke 101
Baird, Julia 156
Balmoral 112–15, *157*
Beatrice, Princess 146
  at Victoria's funeral 9, 10
  censors Victoria's diaries 11
  birth of 133–4
  marriage to Prince Henry 173–4, 177
  at Victoria's death 183
Bedchamber Crisis 55–63
Bedford, Duchess of 92
Benson, Arthur 11
Bigge, Sir Arthur 62, 177
Black, Jack 140
Boehm, Joseph 151, 163
Boer War 181
Branden, Lord 44
Brown, John 173
  and Victoria's funeral 9
  memorials to destroyed 10
  first accompanies Victoria 140
  relationship with Victoria 153–63
Bruce, Henry 159
Brunel, Isambard Kingdom 140
Buckingham Palace 42–3, 91–2, 106, 139–40
Buren, Martin van 65
Cambridge, Duke of 120
Canning, Lady 135
Canning, Lord 135
Caroline of Brunswick, Queen 14
Charles, Prince of Leiningen 16, 32, 35, 133–4
Charlotte, Princess of Wales 14–15, 23, 24
Charlotte, Queen 15
Charlotte of Mecklenberg-Strelitz, Queen 13, 16
Chartist movement 119–20
Christian of Schleswig-Holstein, Prince 149, 151, 180
Christian Victor, Prince 181
Churchill, Lady Jane 181, 183
Claremont House 23–4
Clarendon, Lord 138
Clark, Sir James 55–6, 57, 58, 63, 95, 133
Clarke, Sir Charles 57
Clémentine, Princess 118
Cole, Henry 122
Conroy, Sir John 19, *27*, 47–8
  control of Victoria's early life 25–6, 28, 31, 32, 33, 34–5
  dismissed from Victoria's household 39, 41
  becomes gentleman farmer 48
  and Lady Flora Hastings 56
Constitutional History of England (Hallam) 82
Conyngham, Lord 37
Court Doctor Dissected, The 63
Creevey, Thomas 48, 52–3

Crimean War 126–9, 131
Crystal Palace 122–4
Cubitt, Thomas 106
'Cumberland Plot' 25–6, 28
Derby, Lord 128, 146
Diamond Jubilee celebrations 177–80
Dickens, Charles 51–2, 76
Disraeli, Benjamin
  at coronation of Victoria 50
  relationship with Victoria 149–50, 169–70
  death of 160
  and Empress of India title 169
Economist, The 187–8
Edward, Prince
  early behaviour 15–16
  marriage to Princess Victoria 16, 18
  and birth of Queen Victoria 18, 19
  death of 19
Edward VII, King (Bertie) *182*
  at Victoria's funeral 9
  orders John Brown memorials destroyed 10
  behaviour as king 11
  birth of 94
  portrait painted by Winterhalter 108
  childhood of 111
  relationship with mother 137–8, 176
  Albert's concerns over 143–4
  blamed for Albert's death 144, 145, 146
  marriage to Queen Alexandra 146–7
  scandals around 171, 180
  falls ill 171, 173
  assassination attempt 181
  at Victoria's death 183, 184
Edward VIII, King 9
Elphinstone, Lord 30–1
Emich Charles, Prince 16
Ernest, Duke of Cumberland 15, 24, 28, 38, 85–6
Ernest, Prince 15, 104
Ernest II, Duke of Saxe-Coburg and Gotha 31, 66, 68, 70, 104
Ernst I, Prince 20
Esher, Lord 11
Eugénie, Empress 171
Examiner 51
Feodora of Leiningen, Princess 9, 16, 20, 21, 23, 38, 45, 141, 152
Fitzgerald, Hamilton 57, 58
Fitzherbert, Maria 14
Flowers, Thomas 50
Frederica Charlotte, Princess 15
Frederica of Mecklenberg-Strelitz, Princess 15
Frederick, Duke of York 15
Frederick, Prince of Wales 13
Frederick III, Kaiser 133, 135–6, 147, 150, 176
Friedrich of Hesse and by Rhine, Prince 173
Galsworthy, John 7
George I, King 13
George II, King 13
George III, King 13–16, 42
George IV, King 14, 18, 21, 42

George V, King 10, 15
Gladstone, William 149, 150, 159, 160, 164
Golden Jubilee celebrations 174–6
Gordon, Sir Robert 113
Graf zu Solms, Alexander 70
Great Exhibition 122–4
Greville, Charles 52, 101, 114
Halford, Sir Henry 32
Hallam, Henry 82
Hanstein, Alexander von 70
Harald, Prince 173
Hardinge, Lord Charles 157
Hastings, Lady Flora 55–9, 62, 63
Hastings, Lord 63
Helena, Princess
  at Victoria's funeral 10
  birth of 110
  relationship with mother 138–9
  marriage to Prince Christian 149, 151
  death of Prince Harald 173
  charity work 176, 180
  death of children 180
  at Victoria's death 183
Helena of Waldeck and Pyrmont, Princess 171, 180
Henry of Battenberg, Prince 173–4, 177
Henry of Prussia, Prince 10
Hilton, Boyd 43
Holland, Lady 53
Holland, Lord 39
Howley, William 37
Indian Mutiny 134–5
Ingestre, Lady Sarah 62
Jeffreys, Lieutenant Colonel 127
Jenkinson, Lady Catherine 34
Jersey, Lady 74
John, Marquess of Lorne 151
Jones, Edward 91
Jordan, Dorothea 15
Karim, Abdul 10, 164–8
Kensington Palace 19–20, 42
'Kensington system' 26, 28–9
Kent, William 20
Kitchener, General 181
Lamb, Caroline 43–4
Lancet, The 63
Landor, Walter Savage 76
Landseer, Sir Edwin 90, 155–6
Lansdowne, Lord 101, 128
Lehzen, Louise 19, 21, 23, 26, 34–5, 50, 56, 68, 94, 95–7, 99, 152
Leopold, Prince
  birth of 124
  relationship with mother 138
  and O'Connor's attack on Victoria 158
  marriage to Princess Helena 171
  death of 173
Leopold I, King 16
  during Victoria's early years 23–4, 30, 31, 33, 35
  and Victoria's accession to throne 38
  and Victoria's marriage to Albert 65, 66, 68

death of 151–2
Leopold II, King 10, 178, 180
Leopold Mountbatten, Lord 174
Lincoln, Abraham 148
Lincoln, Mary 148–9
Lindley, Miss 67
Lipton, Sir Thomas 178
Liverpool, Lord 34–5, 103
Locock, Charles 87
Lorne, Lord 177
Louis of Battenberg, Prince 174
Louis of Hesse-Darmstadt, Prince 146, 150
Louis-Philippe, King 24, 117, 118, 120
Louise, Princess
    at Victoria's funeral 9, 10
    birth of 118–19
    marriage to Marquess of Lorne 151
    paintings exhibited 175–6
    rumours of affairs 177
    and Diamond Jubilee 181
    at Victoria's death 183
Louise of Hesse, Grand Duke 174, 180
Louise Margaret, Princess 171
Louise of Orléans, Princess 24
Louise of Saxe-Gotha-Altenburg, Princess 70
Lutyens, Edwin 151
Lyttelton, Lady 97, 111
Maclean, Roderick 160–2
Marie, Princess 173
Maria Amelia, Queen 118
Marie of Württemberg, Duchess 70
Marochetti, Carlo 145, 175
Mary, Queen 15
Mary of Teck, Princess 177
Maud of Denmark, Princess 10
Mayern, Baron von 70
Melbourne, Lord 26, *40*, 45
    on Prince Edward 19
    preparations for Victoria's accession 34
    and death of William IV 38
    and Victoria's accession to throne 39, 41
    private life of 43, 53
    relationship with Victoria 43–4, 52–3,
       92–3
    at coronation of Victoria 49, 50, 51
    and Bedchamber Crisis 55–63
    and Victoria's marriage to Albert 65–6, 67,
       69, 70, 71, 74, 77, 78
    negotiations over Albert's position 72–3
    and Albert's role after marriage 82–3,
       86–7, 92
    loses 1841 general election 92–3, 94
    and sacking of Louise Lehzen 97
Melcy, Monsieur de 67
Mendelssohn, Felix 110
Michael, Tsarevich 10
Montefiore, Moses 44
Montrose, Duchess of 62
Mordaunt, Harriet 171
Morning Post 59
Napier, Sir Charles 62–3
Napoleon III, Emperor 171
Nash, John 42

Newcastle, Duke of 127–8
Nicholas I, Tsar 61
Nicholas II, Tsar 177
Nightingale, Florence 128
Normandy, Lady 92
Norton, Caroline 44, 53
O'Connor, Arthur 156–9
O'Connor, Feargus 158
O'Farrell, Henry James 150
Osborne House 106, 108–10
Oxford, Edward 84–6
Palmerston, Lord 32, 128–9
Pate, Robert 122
Peel, Sir Robert 41
    resignation of 60–1, 110
    relationship with Albert 93, 100
    and Osborne House 106
    death of 120
Phipps, Sir C. 155
Ponsonby, Henry 163, 167
Portman, Lady Emma 56–7
Profeit, Alexander 156
Raglan, Lord 128
Reid, Sir James 156, 165, 168, 183, 184
Richmond, Duke of 67
Roberts, Lord 181
Rolle, Lord 50
Rosebery, Lord 64
Royal Marriages Act (1772) 14
Russell, Lord John 101
    and Melbourne's resignation 60
    negotiations over Albert's position 72
    asked to become Prime Minister 128
    and Victoria's reaction to Albert's death 149
St Helier, Lady 7
Sainte-Laurent, Julie 16
Salisbury, Lord 164, 175
Sanger, George 111
Satirist, The 76
Seven Weeks' War 150–1
Sheridan, Charles 67
Smith, John 114
Smith, William 114
Sophia, Princess 15
Späth, Baroness 26
Spectator, The 47, 71
Stanhope, Lady 53
Stockmar, Baron von 33, 38, 39, 68, 95,
    96, 97
Strachey, Lytton 83
Sutherland, Duchess of 92, 147
Tennyson, Alfred Lord 145–6, 159, 163
Thumb, Tom 104–5
Times, The 21, 44, 158
Victoire, Princess 118
Victoria, Empress 10
Victoria, Princess Royal
    birth of 86–8
    relationship with parents 88–90
    cared for by Louise Lehzen 94–5
    marriage to Kaiser Friedrich 133, 135–6
    birth of Wilhelm II 136–7
    relationship with mother 136–7

unpopularity in Prussia 176
breast cancer 180
Victoria, Queen
  funeral 7–10
  as national figurehead 10–11
  birth of 18–19
  early childhood 19–24
  starts diary 21
  influence of Sir John Conroy on 25–6, 28
  under 'Kensington system' 26, 28–9
  and William IV's coronation 30
  first meetings with Albert 30–1
  growing independence 31–3
  and William IV's ill-health 34–5
  and death of William IV 37–8
  accession to throne 39, 41
  work ethic 41–2
  move to Buckingham Palace 42–3
  relationship with Lord Melbourne 43–4,
    52–3, 92–3, 94
  defies conventions 44–5
  early popularity of 47–8
  coronation of 48–51
  admiration of Charles Dickens 51–2
  and Bedchamber Crisis 55–63
  decides to marry Prince Albert 65–9
  love for Albert 69–72
  negotiations over Albert's position
  wedding day 74–9
  early married life 81–2
  Albert's role after marriage 82–4, 86,
    91–3, 99–101, 124, 131–2
  assassination attempt on 84–6
  birth of daughter Victoria 87–8
  relationship with daughter Victoria 88–90
  control of life in Buckingham Palace 91–2
  sacking of Louise Lehzen 94, 95–7, 99
  birth of Edward VII 94
  flexibility of 100–1
  birth of Alice 103
  meets Tom Thumb 104–5
  first separation from Albert 105–6
  birth of Alfred 106
  at Osborne House 108–10
  birth of Helena 110
  lowbrow tastes of 110–11
  at Balmoral 112–15
  fear of 1848 revolutions 117–19, 120
  birth of Louise 118–19
  birth of Arthur 120
  attacked with cane 120–2
  birth of Leopold 124
  outbursts at Albert 124–6
  reconciled with mother 126
  concerns over Crimean War 126–9
  celebrates Alberts 35th birthday 132–3
  birth of Beatrice 133–4
  relationship with children 134, 137–9,
    151, 171, 173–4
  and Indian Mutiny 134–5
  marriage of Princess Victoria 135–6
  during Great Stink 139–40
  death of mother 140–1

death of Albert 144–6
withdraws from public life 146–9
return to public life 149–50
relationship with Benjamin Disraeli 149–50
relationship with William Gladstone 150,
  164
difficulties over Seven Weeks' War 150–1
death of Leopold I 151–2
relationship with John Brown 153–63
attacked by Arthur O'Connor 156–9
assassination attempt in Windsor 160–2
relationship with Abdul Karim 164–8
and British Empire 169–70
influence on European affairs 170–1
Golden Jubilee celebrations 174–6
Diamond Jubilee celebrations 177–80
and Second Boer War 181
final illness and death 181, 183–6
Victoria Eugénie, Princess 175
Victoria Eugénie, Queen 174
Victoria of Saxe-Coburg-Sallfield, Duchess
  17
  marriage to Prince Edward 16, 18
  and birth of Queen Victoria 19
  rumoured affair with John Conroy 25–6
  relationship with William IV 30
  and Victoria's growing independence 31,
    32, 33, 34–5
  and Victoria's accession to throne 41, 47–8
  and Bedchamber Crisis 56, 57, 58, 62
  and Victoria's marriage to Albert 69, 74,
    76, 77
  reconciled with Victoria 126
  death of 140–1
Viktoria, Princess 176
Waldemar, Prince 173
Waterpark, Lady Eliza Jane 148, 152
Wellington, Duke of
  and Victoria's accession to throne 39
  and John Conroy 48
  declines chance to become Prime Minister
    60
  negotiations over Albert's position 72
  and Albert's role after marriage 84, 86
  and Chartist movement 119
Wilhelm I, Kaiser 133, 171
Wilhelm II, Kaiser
  at Victoria's funeral 9
  birth of 136–7
  at Golden Jubilee celebrations 176
  at Victoria's death 183, 184
William III, King 19
William IV, King
  children of 15, 18
  in line to throne 18
  John Conroy's opinion of 26
  letter to Victoria 32
  ill-health 32, 34–5
  death of 37–8
William of Löwenstein, Prince 82
Windsor Castle 106, 107, 139–40
Winterhalter, Franz 108, 132, 137
Wren, Christopher 20